The Relevance of Biblical Prophecy

The Relevance of Biblical Prophecy

Lance Lambert

LANCE LAMBERT MINISTRIES

Richmond, Virginia, USA

ISBN: 978-1-68389-112-3

www.lancelambert.org

Contents

Introduction

At the Christian Family Conference, given in Richmond, Virginia in 1982, Lance shared a series of messages on the relevance of Biblical prophecy. These messages have been edited only for clarity. The timeliness of these messages is just as relevant in today's day as it was then in 1982.

1.
An Understanding of Biblical Prophecy

I Thessalonians 5:1–11

But concerning the times and the seasons, brethren, ye have no need that aught be written unto you. For yourselves know perfectly that the day of the Lord so cometh as a thief in the night. When they are saying, Peace and safety, then sudden destruction cometh upon them as travail upon a woman with child; and they shall in no wise escape. But ye, brethren, are not in darkness that that day should overtake you as a thief: for ye are all sons of light, and sons of the day: we are not of the night, nor of darkness; so then let us not sleep, as do the rest, but let us watch and be sober. For they that sleep sleep in the night; and they that are drunken are drunken in the night. But let us, since we are of the day, be sober, putting on the breastplate of faith and love; and for a helmet, the hope of salvation. For God appointed us not unto wrath, but unto the obtaining of salvation through our Lord Jesus Christ, who died for us, that, whether we wake or sleep, we should live together with Him. Wherefore exhort one

another, and build each other up, even as also ye do.

Shall we just bow together in the word of prayer?

Father, as we turn to You this morning, we want to praise You and worship You that You have given us all the grace and the power that we need, both for speaking and for hearing and Lord, we just commit ourselves into Your hands. We pray, oh Lord, that Your Word may find a dwelling place in our hearts. We thank You for everything that You have done thus far in our week together in Your presence, and we ask now for this morning Lord. We don't take it for granted. We just come by faith to lay hold of that provision which You have made for every one of us, that whether speaker or hearer, we may know Your divine enabling and power so that, Lord, Your purpose for this time may be fulfilled, and we ask this together in the name of our Lord Jesus. Amen.

In these times, I have a responsibility to share with you the word of God and the matter that has been in my heart has been this whole matter of Biblical prophecy. Now, don't get all excited because I am not going to talk and spend the time on all the many controversial and difficult matters to do with the things of the end, yet we shall take up some of those matters. This whole matter of Biblical prophecy is a matter of tremendous complexity, and upon it, centred on it, has been much controversy. There is much confusion over it. There is not a little error, and imbalance, and eccentricity, and yet, there is no subject which is more vital, more strategic, more important for the people of God to understand and to have light upon than this matter of Biblical prophecy. We are moving irreversibly into the last days of the age, and more than at any other time, as the people of God, we need to understand the word of prophecy. We need to have an understanding of the times in which we live.

Considering Prophecy or Considering the Word of Prophecy

It is not good enough for God's people to be kind of spiritual escapists. Thinking, "Well, we are going to be with the Lord and that is the only thing that matters because the rest of the world is going to hell. The rest of the world is under judgment. After we have gone, they will suffer unspeakable horrors and terrible things, but thank God we are not going to be there. All we have to do is withdraw from the world and worship the Lord and read His Word. We are going to escape all of it."

Now, I believe, personally, that the Lord is going to come for His own, and I believe it is essential that we should be ready for His coming. Nor do I think for a single moment that some kind of morbid, dark, heavy, afflicted kind of spirit should come upon us, or that we should start to look at the Antichrist, and 666, and all of that, such as the antichrist system that is going to come, and the suffering and persecution that the people of God will face and all these things. I mean, to be morbid would be very sad.

The apostle Paul, writing to the Thessalonians, put it in beautiful words, he said, "God appointed us not unto wrath, but unto the obtaining of salvation through our Lord Jesus Christ, who died for us, that, whether we wake or sleep, we should live together with Him. Wherefore, exhort one another and build each other up even as also ye do," (1 Thessalonians 5:9–11).

It is an interesting thing that whenever the Word of God has to define for us or paint for us a picture of reality, a picture sometimes in dark colours, of unpleasant things, the Holy Spirit without fail always reveals the Lord Jesus as the enthroned Lamb, or the coming glory of the kingdom of God, or the wonderful deliverance of those who belong to Him, or the fulfilment of the whole purpose of God for the creation and for mankind. It is marvellous to remember these things. Of course, the Lord Jesus put it very simply in those words, "When you see these things beginning to come to pass, look up, lift up your heads, for your redemption draweth nigh," (Luke 21:28).

Our Response

Now, this is interesting because I have just made reference to the fact that we can be kind of spiritual escapists—just blessing the Lord in a holy huddle, just waiting for the Lord to come, and not bothering about the world around us, or what is happening in the world or what is happening to the people in it. It is interesting that the Lord Jesus said, "When you see these things beginning to come to pass, look up, lift up your heads for your redemption draweth nigh." Now, to stand up, to look up, to lift up your heads is the Jewish form of worship. What the Lord Jesus was saying is: Be so unconcerned about all these terrible things that you will be able to worship the Lord because your redemption is drawing nearer every day. You can lift up your head, you can straighten your back, you can stand up together in the presence of the Lord, and you can worship Him because your redemption is drawing near.

Now in this passage that we read together, the Holy Spirit through the apostle Paul speaks of this day in verse 2: "For yourselves know perfectly that the day of the Lord so cometh as a thief in the night."

The Lord Jesus Himself referred to His coming as being like that of a thief in the night. He said this in Matthew 24:43–44: "But know this, that if the master of the house had known in what watch the thief was coming, he would have watched, and would not have suffered his house to be broken through. Therefore be ye also ready; for in an hour that ye think not the Son of man cometh."

The Lord Jesus did not say this to a lot of unsaved people. He did not actually utter these words to a great multitude of unsaved people. He did not even say these words to the great company of His disciples. He did not even say these words to the twelve disciples that were the inner circle. He said these words to the most devoted and the most responsible of the twelve: Andrew, Peter, James, and John, that inner circle of the inner circle that again and again He took with Him on special occasions. When Jairus's daughter was raised it was three of these, when the transfiguration took place, it was three of these and so on and so forth. In other words, I don't know about you, but it comes to me with some solemnity that the Lord Jesus was speaking to the most responsible of His servants and said, "I will come like a thief that can catch out even those most responsible in My work and in the interests of My kingdom. Therefore, be ye also ready for in an hour that you think not, the Son of man comes."

Now, don't you think the Lord Jesus was seeking, as it were, to get something over to us? We may have a great knowledge of the Word of God, we may have responsibility in the things of God, we may have a long history in the work of God, and yet, according to the words of the Lord Jesus, we could be caught out by the coming of the Lord.

It is interesting that in Revelation 16:15, the Lord Jesus again refers to His coming, "Behold I come as a thief. Blessed is he that watcheth, and keepeth his garments, lest he walk naked, and they see his shame." I think in the New International Version it says, "Lest he be shamefully exposed." Is it possible for a believer to lose his garments? To, as it were, be naked, to be found out and be shamefully exposed by the coming of the Lord Jesus? If it is not a possibility, why does the Lord Jesus continuously warn us to be ready?

Be Ye Ready

People get so excited about whether we are going to go before the tribulation, after the tribulation, or in the midst of the tribulation, whether we are all going to go or whether just a few of us are going to go, whether those who are ready are going to go, and all the rest of it. They get so heated, so upset on the details about the coming of the Lord and all-together forget the main emphasis of our Lord Jesus, "Therefore be ye also ready; for in an hour that you think not the Son of man cometh." If our Lord Jesus, not once, but again and again and again, spoke of taking heed, watching, being alert, being on our guard, being ready, there must be some kind of spiritual loss if we ignore his advice.

It is a most striking term that Jesus and the apostles use, "a thief, like a thief in the night." There is nothing about the Lord Jesus remotely akin to a thief. If He had not Himself used the illustration, it would be offensive and vulgar. If I had taken it upon myself to speak about the coming of the Lord Jesus as being like a thief in the night, many people would have got up, I think, and walked out. They would have been disgusted that someone could refer to the Lord Jesus as a thief! Yet, it was the Lord Jesus Himself who spoke of His coming as being like a thief, not even a businessman. (Some of them are thieves, but never mind.) If He had said a businessman, it would have at least been a bit more respectable. If He had said a politician (some of those are swindlers too) but He would have at least been a little more respectable. But to have baldly stated, "My coming will be like a thief in the night." Thieves do not telephone you beforehand and say, "At such-and-such a time I will be paying you a visit." Thieves do not send in a visiting card first, "Mr. So-and-So is coming: thief!" The very nature of thieving is to do it suddenly, stealthily, in a hidden manner!

In other words, what the Lord Jesus is warning us, not once, but again and again (and the apostles support this warning), His coming will be like a thief, stealthy, hidden, unseen, unexpected. Most of us would think, "Now, I will not be caught out. I know the Lord." Some of you will say, "I, actually, am very interested in prophecy, so I do not think I will be caught out. Oh, I wish this kind of word would come to the church I am in or the company I am in, or the brothers and sisters I meet with ..." However, it was to Andrew, Peter, James, and John that the Lord Jesus said, "If the master of the house had known at what watch the thief would come, he would have kept watch! He would not have suffered the thief to have broken through into his house. Be ye also ready for in an hour that you think not the Son of man comes."

This matter of Biblical prophecy is not a matter to be despised. I know that this subject has attracted to it like a magnet eccentrics of extraordinary dimensions and vividness. We, of course, see them very much in Jerusalem. That draws them more than any other place. But just because eccentrics are attracted to a subject does not invalidate the truth of the prophetic word. After all, salvation has attracted some eccentrics, we all know them, and there are extremes sometimes, imbalance sometimes in the teaching. If you and I are so easily put off by a few erroneous teachings, or by a few imbalanced teachings, or by the antics of eccentrics in this matter, we shall be so at great loss to ourselves. That, in fact, in my estimation, is the very strategy of hell. It is: if it cannot stop the people of God from understanding the prophetic word, the word of prophecy, if it cannot stop that word of prophecy from being a lamp to the feet of God's people, a lamp shining in a dark and squalid place, giving them light, giving them direction, giving them understanding, then Satan and his forces will seek to discredit the subject in such a way and to such a degree that most sane believers will be altogether put off by the matter. This means that you and I can then be left bereft of the one means that God would use to give us an understanding of the days in which we live and awaken us to the danger in which we as the people of God are found.

So, dear people of God this whole matter of biblical prophecy is not something which can be put on one side, which can be ignored. It is not a special subject, which is left to those who have got a feeling for it. This is a subject of tremendous and strategic importance for the people of God, and particularly for the last days in which we are found. I say this again as emphatically as I can. The simple fact of the matter is, that we not only need to know the broad outlines of God's purpose, the fact of our salvation, the fulness of our salvation, the nature of the church, the destiny of the church, and these tremendous matters if we are going to be a functioning church or believers that are really overcoming in the final phase of world history, but we must also have an understanding of what is happening amongst the nations.

God, as the God of History

God is not only the God of the redeemed, but He is also the God of all nations, the God of all flesh. This is why there will be a great final judgment. Every single human being will stand before God, great and small, no matter if they have been incinerated, no matter if they have been drowned, no matter if they have been dead for five or six-thousand years. Every single human being will finally stand before God because God is the God of all flesh.

God is the God of history. He is not just interested in His people only. Of course, He is interested in His people, supremely interested in His people. They are the apple of His eye. They are the bride of His Son. They are that new Jerusalem. They are His home in the spirit. They are the heart of the matter, the pivotal centre of a whole new heaven and new earth in which righteousness will dwell. Of course, He is supremely interested in His people. But dear people of God, do not think for a single moment that God is an unknown factor in the Kremlin. They may be atheists, but God, if I may so speak of Him, walks the chambers of the Kremlin and the corridors of the Kremlin. There is not a conversation that is not heard by God and noted by God. He is no stranger to the White House, or to the Capitol, or to the Houses of Parliament in Britain, or to the Knesset in Israel. He hears everything, takes note of everything, and is working everything out according to the counsel of His own will. Nothing happens by accident. This should be a tremendous encouragement to the people of God!

It is not as if the Lord is only interested in the church and the redeemed and has thrown up the rest and has said. "They can get on with it; I could not care less." This is the spirit of Jonah. When the Lord said to Jonah, "Go to Nineveh," Jonah said, "Never! Not on your life. Go to that cruel, wicked lot who have done the most barbaric things in the whole of human history and preach to them? Certainly not." He fled before the Lord could say another word to him, down to Joppa, onto a boat. And the Lord prepared for him a great fish. (I think you know the story). In the end, Jonah ended up in that great fish and had an extraordinary prayer meeting!

I have often thought of the prayer meeting that Jonah had in that great fish as one of the most amazing prayer meetings in history. For instance, he remembered the words of King Solomon: "If anyone, anywhere," (anywhere!) "on the earth should turn toward the place where I have caused my name to dwell, I will hear him and forgive him." I have often thought, How did Jonah, in the belly of a fish, know in which direction Jerusalem was and the fish might have been churning around in circles. I take it that Jonah said, "Lord, you know my heart. I am turning towards Jerusalem, at least, the direction I *think* Jerusalem is in. Take it as if I am facing the place where You have caused Your name to dwell" and God heard him and the fish was beached and coughed up Jonah. You remember the story.

Then the Lord said, "Now Jonah, I was saying to you a few days ago, about going to Nineveh" and Jonah said, "Yes, Lord, I will go to Nineveh. Since it obviously means so much to you, Lord, I will go to Nineveh."

God sometimes has to take some of us through so much before finally we hear His word and are finally prepared to be obedient. Jonah came to Nineveh, but now unfortunately, Jonah threw himself too much into his message. It was a message of judgment! It exactly fitted Jonah's mood, and he spoke with not only his spirit, but with *all* his soul. He spoke powerfully and had the shock of his life. Jonah had ministered for quite a few years in Israel, but never had the king put on sackcloth and thrown ashes on himself and wept before God. Never had the people of the northern kingdom of Israel ever humbled themselves before God and dressed even their cattle in black and wept before the Lord and fasted before the Lord. But the royal house in Nineveh and the whole royal court mourned and fasted before God as if someone had died. God said to Jonah, "Jonah, I cannot do this thing!" You know the story. Jonah got very upset indeed. He said, "Lord, I knew you would do this to me! You sent me all this way with this message of judgment to this ghastly people. They should be destroyed to the last man. I had a funny, sneaking suspicion all the while that if I gave this message and they as much as wept a tear, You would put the whole thing off for a generation."

Many of us are just like Jonah. We are perfectly prepared to pronounce a kind of judgment upon the world around us, but we do not want to be involved. We do not believe that God knows the streets of Nineveh, that He knows every single family in Nineveh, that He could speak of the thousands of little children, kindergarten age, who did not know their left hand from their right hand. Do you remember the words with which the Lord ended His talk with Jonah? I am sure He said a lot more to Jonah, but it took a great man of great spiritual character to write the record and leave himself in such a dark painting. The Lord said to Jonah, "Jonah, do you mean to tell Me that you want Me to judge this city? What about the little ones who cannot tell their left hand from their right hand and what about the cattle?" I think it was the biggest shock Jonah ever had. He said, "Lord, You are interested in the domestic animals in this city? Jerusalem I can understand. Everything in Jerusalem is precious to the Lord, but *Nineveh*?"

Being a Prophetic Community

We are in a situation very much like this, in a world that is moving steadily towards the judgments of God and we, as the people of God, are to be a prophetic community. What do I mean? I mean this: the church is not a matter essentially of pattern, of offices, of functions, of gifts. All these things are necessary, but you can have *all* of that and there is no lampstand there. It has been removed. The lampstand speaks of something more. It speaks of the light of the life of God in the Lord Jesus. The lampstand holds a lamp and in the lamp is light. Jesus is the lamp, the glory of God is the light in that lamp, and the church is the lampstand that holds the lamp—Christ in you, plural, you all, the hope of glory.

You know, the church should be a prophetic community. What do I mean? I mean that the church should be a community of redeemed people who are a prophetic instrument in the area in which they are found. Let me put it another way. It is not just that they have a knowledge of prophecies. It is much, much, much more than that. It is not only that they have an understanding of the prophetic word, but the prophetic word has come *into* them. Something has come right inside of these people and they are acting according to the word of God.

Jesus spoke of us as the salt of the earth. There is a fatalistic attitude amongst the people of God that the moral decline and wickedness in the nation is something that we as the people of God can do absolutely nothing about. But we are the salt of the earth! In other words, it is not just simply the truth we proclaim, but the truth that is in us which acts like an antiseptic. It acts like an agent that halts the corruption. We are the light of the world. In other words, the church is to be an instrument through which the light of God streams into a locality, or into a town, or village, or a city, into a nation, and any man or woman who wants to know the truth can find God through that light shining through the church. The church is to be a city set on a hill. You cannot hide a city set on a hill. The truth is there in action for *all* to see.

Brother Stephen Kaung referred to that verse in the most wonderful way in Revelation 19:10b where it says, "the testimony of Jesus is the spirit of prophecy." I do not think that the way it is sometimes explained, as meaning the prophetic scriptures all point to Jesus, is a satisfactory interpretation of that statement. Of course, it includes that, but it is much, much more. In my estimation, it means this: the church which holds the testimony of Jesus and the Word of God, this testimony of Jesus is prophetic in its content. The church is meant to have an impact upon the world, upon the nation in which it lives. This does not mean that you all become politicians or that you all spend all your time in agitating for reforms of one kind or another. However, it does mean this: that the people of God should stand up and be accounted because they have a responsibility to God.

Do not think for one single moment that any believer has only a responsibility for his own spiritual welfare and well-being, as if the only thing Christ will ask you when you stand before His judgment seat is, "What did you do about your own character? What did you do about your own well-being? How did you secure spiritual values in your life?" Of course, He will be interested in that, but that is not *all*. The Lord Jesus will say to you, "What kind of responsibility did you have for your brothers and sisters? Did you care for them? Did you wash their feet? Did you humble yourself before them? Did you love them? Did you dress them? Did you feed them? Did you heal them? Did you lay down your lives for your brothers and sisters? You talk so much about the building of the house of God, so much about the church of God, but what have *you* done concerning your brothers and sisters, not on the other side of the world, but where you live?"

"I Have Made You A Watchman"

Do not think that is all. The Lord Jesus will then say to you, "You are a watchman. I set you on the walls of Jerusalem. I gave you in My word, warning of what would happen to the world. Did you at any time pray for that world around you? Did you give yourself in intercession for those souls, those multitudes of souls that were going into a lost eternity? Did you become a prophetic instrument with others by which My light could stream? Did you warn them? Did you blow the trumpet? Did you sound the alarm?"

Do you know what God said to the prophet Ezekiel? He said, "I have made you a watchman. If you sound the alarm when I say that judgment is coming and they take no note of you and they die, you have saved yourself and those ones will die in judgment. Their blood is upon their own head. But if I say that you should sound the alarm and blow the trumpet because judgment is coming, and you do not do anything but spend your time in a holy huddle, when the judgment comes upon that nation I will require their blood at your hand!"

You are responsible! It is not only for your own spiritual well-being, not only for the building up and the recovery of the church, but for the nation and nations amongst whom you are placed.

You may say to me, "Well, I do not know much about the word of prophecy, the prophetic word. I have never really taken too much account of it." Well, my dear friend, let me say this straightaway, whether you have ignored it or whether you have regarded it, it has been given to you. You and I have a solemn responsibility before God, so this matter of biblical prophecy is vital.

You see, it was bad enough centuries ago, but now we are on the brink of God's judgments upon the nations. We are on the brink of all kinds of things that will come upon the face of the earth. Which people, amongst all the peoples in the earth, which people have got understanding if it is not the church of our Lord Jesus? Therefore, we have this responsibility and before I finish, I would like to just say something about the meaning of prophecy.

A Seer

There are several words that are used in Hebrew and they all help us to understand what it means. We have two words that are akin in Hebrew. One is *ro'e* and the other *h oze* and these two words mean, "a prophet is a seer." They come from a root that just means, "To see." A prophet is nothing less and nothing more than a man who sees God, and in seeing God he understands everything else. What he sees of the mind and the heart of God means that his whole attitude to human and earthly events undergoes a change. If you want scriptures for that you will find them in 1 Samuel 9:9 and Isaiah 30:10 for those of you who want to look it up.

There are, of course, many, many more references all the way through the Old Testament with this word concerning the prophet. He is called a "seer;" one who sees. He does not cook up ideas in his head. He does not gaze into some crystal ball and get some ideas of the future. It is not tea leaf divination, or palm reading, or anything like that. It is not looking at the stars. He sees the Lord and that marks him out from all these other kinds of occult, magical things that belong to Satan and to this earth. He and she see the Lord and because they see the Lord, they speak.

Called and Commissioned by God

There is another word that is used most commonly of all, it is the word *nabiy*[1] in Hebrew. There is much discussion about where this word came from. Some say it comes from a Hebrew root which means "to announce." A prophet is someone who announces the mind of God. He sees the Lord and he announces, he declares what he sees. There are others who say it comes from an Assyrian word, the root *nabu* "to be called." They say this prophet, this *nabiy'* is someone who is called of God, and that is true. No man can be a prophet simply because he thinks he will be a prophet; we have got plenty of them. The Bible calls them false prophets. They announce things they were not told to announce. They say they are prophets when they have never been called by God. The prophet is called and commissioned by God.

The Burden of the Lord

There is another word used in Hebrew which is a little different to the others. It's used in association with the prophet. It is a word that means "burden." This other word you will find in Zechariah 9:1, Zechariah 12:1, Malachi 1:1. You read there, "The burden of the Lord, which He gave to so-and-so," and this is a very interesting

1 See Genesis 20:7 or Numbers 11:29 for the word *nabiy'*

word in Hebrew, *massa'*. Desired destination. It speaks of the revelation that God gives to a prophet being a divine burden or load that God lifts up and puts, as it were, upon the shoulders, or the heart, of the prophet so that that word may achieve God's desired end.

In the New Testament we have one common word used throughout. *Prophētēs* from which we get the words in English, "prophet" and "prophecy." It simply means one who speaks forth, or speaks out, or tells forth.

Forth-Telling—Past, Present, Future

Here we come to the heart of this whole matter of biblical prophecy. It is not just predicting the future as so many imagine. It is not just summing up, foretelling what is going to happen. It is the speaking out of the mind and the heart of God. It is the forth-telling of the mind and the heart of God. Do you understand? It can be to do with the past, and the present, and the future. Sometimes a prophet will say to a people, for example, "So many centuries ago you did this and that is why this is happening." Only a prophet could have said that. He has put the finger of God, as it were, upon a matter which is the root of all the problem in that nation or in that community. It is to do with the past. Now in the Scripture you will find a lot of prophecy about the past. Do you remember the amazing prophecy about Lucifer, son of the morning, falling down? The anointed cherub who has said, "I will be like the Most High, I will ascend to the stars, I will make my throne above the throne of God." (See Isaiah

14:13, 14). That is prophetic! Human intelligence could never have understood that! Going to a university or a theological seminary would not have produced that. That could only come by revelation! So again, and again, and again, prophecy is to do with the past.

It is to do with present. Sometimes God says, "If you do so and so, and so and so, and so and so forth—you need not fear. You will find My deliverance is with you." Do you remember King Jehoshaphat? When they were surrounded and besieged, the Lord said, "Do not take any notice of them. Just worship Me and trust Me. I am with you. Take your position, stand still, and see the salvation of the Lord," (II Chronicles 20:17) and it is exactly what happened! It was something to do with the present situation! The Lord was saying, "If you do so and so, and so and so, and so and so, you will be absolutely safe and secure." That is prophetic.

Then, of course, we have quite a lot to do with the future. It is interesting. Here are some facts for some of you. Out of the 31,124 verses of the Bible, 8,362 are predictive! Now, maybe that does not mean anything to you. You all may be asleep on the point. Let me put it another way: 27% of the Bible is to do with prediction! Now, do you mean to tell me you are going to ignore over *one quarter* of your Bible?

"Well," you say, "I do not like this kind of subject. I feel it belongs to the realm of cranks and lunatics, the lunatic fringe of Christianity." So, we are going to sacrifice 27% of the Bible! Now, I am talking about predictive material. If you take what we call the prophetic word, then we must take a very much larger percentage of the Bible when we are dealing with the past, and with the present, as well as with the future.

Declaring the End from the Beginning

You know, it is a wonderful thing for us. Listen to me in this matter. Let me read to you Isaiah 46:9–11:

> *Remember the former things of old: for I am God, and there is none else; I am God, and there is none like me; declaring the end from the beginning, and from ancient times things that are not yet done; saying, My counsel shall stand, and I will do all my pleasure; calling a ravenous bird from the east, the man of my counsel from a far country; yea, I have spoken, I will also bring it to pass; I have purposed, I will also do it.*

Now, do you not see how marvellously comforting it can be that God declares the end from the beginning?

Well, I do not know about you; I do not know what kind of minds you have. I find mine works overtime, and I have the kind of mind that is all the time wondering, "Is it really true?" But now I am just opening my heart to you. I find again and again the devil comes to me and says, "You do not believe all that rubbish, do you? Really? You believe it?" Sometimes I think to myself, "Just supposing, just supposing that it was nonsense. What on earth have I been doing with my life?"

Now, maybe none of you have such dark thoughts, but I find they are with me day and night. I have learnt to live with them. I just let the devil do his little war dance all around me all the time he wants to. Telling me, "This is wrong. This won't happen and this and this and this." I come back again and again to one or two things that I cannot explain away, not in any single degree can I explain it away. One of the things is this: God has said things thousands of years ago that are being specifically, accurately fulfilled *before my eyes* in a detailed manner. Every time the devil comes to me, I think to myself, "If God can say things like that thousands of years ago, more accurate and more relevant than the *Washington Post* or the *New York Times*, I, for one, can trust God." When people throw the whole thing overboard and only want a kind of mystical, spiritual experience of the Lord they say, "Oh, no, no, no. God isn't fulfilling anything today. No, no, no, no, we just have to walk by faith." It's nonsense.

Moses had to walk by faith when he went through the Red Sea, but God told him they'd get through it. There was a land into which God was going to bring them. He had to walk by faith. There was no other way for that Sea to be divided into two, and for those people to walk over as on dry ground, but God had already declared the end from the beginning. He said, "One day, when you get into that land, I will bring you to a place where I shall cause My name to dwell. There you shall worship Me, and there you shall offer your sacrifices to Me." He declared the end from the beginning, but they had to walk by faith all the way through. Where faith collapsed, they stayed in the desert for 40 years, but where faith triumphed, a new generation went over into the land and possessed it. Every single word that God had said came to pass and so it is with you, and with me.

When the enemy comes to me and says, "Oh, I don't think this will happen, or that will happen. Don't you think you're barking up the wrong tree?" (I never talk to the devil if I can help it.

I think it's better to talk with the Lord.) But I always say to the Lord, "You know, Lord, it is a strange thing this coordination of evil. How come everything happens at once?" Have you ever noticed that? I always say, when everything goes wrong—the tank splits, the car breaks down, the dog gets lost, the telephone goes out of order, someone's violently sick, and then you have some neurotic saint descend upon you in the final stages of a nervous breakdown, I say, "Thank God, He's going to do something before long!" I have learnt from bitter experience that when everything goes wrong, something is about to happen. Have you not found that out? I've never found it to be a mistake! I wait and think: "Something's going to happen," and sure enough, somebody gets saved, or somebody gets blessed, or some tremendous breakthrough takes place. I say, "Now, I understand that coordination of evil!" Who coordinated all these things? Who planned the whole thing? God says, on a much bigger scale, "My beloved children, I want to comfort you. You are going to go through all these centuries of time, but I am declaring the end from the beginning, so that when these things come to pass, you may be comforted and may be strengthened."

He says it again in Isaiah 45:21:

Declare ye, and bring it forth; yea, let them take counsel together: who hath showed this from ancient time? who hath declared it of old? have not I, the Lord? and there is no God else besides me, a just God and a Saviour; there is none besides me.

I would like to leave you with II Peter 1:19. We have referred to this verse two or three times although we have not read it:

And we have the word of prophecy made more sure; whereunto
ye do well that ye take heed, as unto a lamp shining in a dark
place, until the day dawn, and the daystar arise in your hearts.

A lamp, the word of prophecy, a lamp shining in a dark place.
The word *dark* here, in the Greek, means "murky or squalid."
I must tell you; I think the age of degeneration in which we
are living is a pretty squalid generation. We are returning to
Corinthian situations. We are reversing slowly but surely back to
the paganism of centuries ago: abortion, homosexuality, sex with
children and animals, and all the other unspeakable things that
belong to a pagan society. That pagan society, so dehumanised
because of its attitude to human life, could pack stadiums
throughout that magnificent Roman world, and watch men kill
each other and roar with delight! This is what we are coming
to again. We have this prophetic word, like a lamp shining in a
squalid place, a murky place.

My dear friends, what point is it having a map or a chart in a
dark place without a light?

Have you ever thought about it? Think! Some people say,
"Oh, but I've got the Bible, I've got the Bible!" My dear friend,
if you don't have a lamp, what is the point? You will be misdirected;
you will stumble or fall. There are things in the way, obstacles,
hindrances over which you will trip, or things in which you will
be ensnared because you have no light to show you the path,
or to show you the obstacles that are in the path.

"A lamp shining in a dark place ..." Thank God for the Word,
but thank God for the prophetic word, which is like a lamp shining
in a squalid place, that can give us light so that we can read the

chart, so that we can see the map, so that we can see where we're going, so we can understand where we have arrived and at what point we are on the journey.

The Word of Prophecy —
"Until the Day Dawns"

Look again at this verse, "We have the word of prophecy made more sure; whereunto ye do well that ye take heed as unto a lamp shining in a dark place, until the day dawn." Until the day dawn!

So, Biblical prophecy is not only relevant to the end of the New Testament age. What nonsense some people speak when they tell me everything ended with the New Testament age. "Everything ended with the New Testament age, never a tongue to be spoken, never a prophecy to be uttered, never a gift to be exercised, it has all ended with the New Testament age." We, dear people of God, are to be left without any ecstasies, without any experiences of the Lord. We are just to go forward like zombies. Is that what it means to walk by faith? I do not think so for a single moment. This says, "Until the day dawn!" In other words, the prophetic word is relevant until the day when the Lord Jesus comes, and the kingdom of God finally arrives publicly. Until that day dawns, this word of prophecy is relevant! Accurate! Trustworthy! Vital!

The Word of Prophecy — "Made More Sure"

Look again at this word. "We have the word of prophecy made *more* sure where unto ye do well that ye take heed..." *Made more sure*. Now, this is quite extraordinary. I am not always so good at English—I mean English English. Of course American English I'm not going to talk about, but English English. Our people tell me, "You shouldn't say that, and you shouldn't say that." Now may I say something? You can't say, "It's made more sure." It's either sure, or it isn't sure. Isn't that so? Either something is certain, or it is not. Now, we speak in a colloquial way about something being more certain, and here, the Spirit of God says, "We have the prophecy made *more* sure!" How can the word of prophecy be made more sure? I tell you because when Peter wrote to these dear people he was saying, "Do you know that a colossal amount of this prophetic word has already been fulfilled?" In other words, you have grounds for even more confidence than the saints who were before you because all these prophecies concerning the Messiah have been fulfilled! We have the prophecy made more sure.

It does not mean, as some people read the King James version, that the New Testament is more sure than the Old Testament. Oh! I don't understand some of them, but they get the idea that the New Testament is more sure than the Old Testament. I want to tell you something, the early church only had an Old Testament and did very well with it. Would to God that the church today with the New Testament and the Old Testament did as well as the New Testament church with only an Old Testament. Well, work that one out. But the thing is this: "made more sure."

Do you know there are 590 major events predicted in the Word and all of them have now been fulfilled except for 20? There are 590 major events and 20 only remain to be fulfilled. We are at the end of the age, whereas when Peter wrote to these people they were at the beginning of the New Testament age. We have the word of prophecy made *even more* sure. Now, this means it's not only relevant, but it means we have confidence! We have a ground for confidence in the Word of God, if God could talk about nations and a nation and peoples and about the church, and these things are being fulfilled before our eyes, do you not think that the things He says about you that He will complete that work in you which He has begun, that He will indeed do it? Don't you think He's going to keep that word if you will trust Him? Do you not think if He says, "My grace is sufficient for you," He means exactly what He says? Of course! Dear people of God, what a wonderful matter we have in this word of prophecy—made more sure.

The Word of Prophecy—"Until the Daystar Arise in Your Hearts"

"The word of prophecy made more sure; whereunto ye do well that ye take heed, as unto a lamp shining in a squalid place, until the day dawn, and," listen, "the *daystar* arise in your hearts."

I have seen the daystar over the mountains of Judah more times than I can remember. Every time I see that great luminous orb hanging there in the darkest part of the night before the morn, I think of the Lord Jesus as the Morning Star. But why does it say the daystar arise in your hearts? Oh, dear people of God, why didn't the Lord say, "Until the daystar arise!"? That would mean the coming of the Lord Jesus, wouldn't it? But He didn't say that, He said, "Until the daystar arise in your hearts!" Could it be that God promises for those who take heed to the word of prophecy, special, intimate, and glorious touches of the Lord

Jesus to enable us to go through this last phase 'til He takes us to be with Himself?

"... 'Til the daystar arise in your hearts!" Thank God, He is going to come, but we need the daystar to arise in our hearts instead of getting all morbid, and frightened about dragons, and serpents, and false prophets, and beasts, and persecution, and what not. People say, "Oh, do not tell us anymore. I did not come to hear that kind of thing. I came to be comforted and strengthened. I did not come to hear dreadful things like that." But the point is this: the daystar can arise in your hearts. Face reality, and let the daystar arise in your heart. Then you will have a touch from God of grace and power that will enable you to go through the last phase until He appears to take us to be with Himself.

Prophecy and Blessing

Let me finally give you this word in Revelation 22:7. The words of the Lord Jesus, "Behold, I come quickly. Blessed is he that keepeth the words of the prophecy of this book." I do not think many believers associate prophecy with blessing. Prophecy is associated with complexity, with having to put a cold pack of ice on your head as you read the different interpretations, prophecy is associated with confusion, sometimes prophecy is associated with fascination. But the Lord Jesus links it to blessing. It is no mistake that the book of Revelation came to its final position as the last book of the Bible. In the last chapter of that book, in almost the concluding words, Jesus says, "Blessed is he that keeps the words of the prophecy of this book." And I think that means not only the book of Revelation but goes right back through the whole Bible to Genesis.

Dear people, if God has really given us a prophetic word to guide us, should we not take heed to it? Should we not now begin to wake up and ask ourselves: "What does this prophetic word really say to us?" We need help from God that we may be alive, alert, on guard, and ready for what is going to happen, and above all for the coming of our Lord Jesus.

Shall we pray?

Lord, will You keep us from any exaggeration of this matter in our minds, or any imbalance, or eccentricity? But Lord stir us up to be a people who begin to take heed to the word of prophecy. Make us a people, Lord, for whom it becomes a lamp shining in a dark, a murky, and a squalid place, giving light, giving us understanding, helping us to avoid the snares and the traps and the obstacles, and giving us an understanding of Your objective and Your end. Dear Lord, we commit ourselves to You. May, in many of our hearts, the Lord Jesus, as the daystar, arise with that brilliance in the darkest part of the night to herald the coming of that day. We ask it in Jesus' name, Amen.

2.
An Outline of World History

Daniel 2:31–45

"Thou, O king, sawest, and, behold, a great image. This image, which was mighty, and whose brightness was excellent, stood before thee; and the aspect thereof was terrible. As for this image, its head was of fine gold, its breast and its arms of silver, its belly and its thighs of brass, its legs of iron, its feet part of iron, and part of clay. Thou sawest till that a stone was cut out without hands, which smote the image upon its feet that were of iron and clay, and brake them in pieces. Then was the iron, the clay, the brass, the silver, and the gold, broken in pieces together, and became like the chaff of the summer threshing-floors; and the wind carried them away, so that no place was found for them; and the stone that smote the image became a great mountain, and filled the whole earth.

This is the dream; and we will tell the interpretation thereof before the king. Thou, O king, art king of kings, unto whom the God of heaven hath given the kingdom, the power, and the strength, and the glory; and wheresoever the children of men dwell, the beasts of the field and the birds of the heavens hath he given into thy hand, and hath made thee to rule over them all: thou art the head of gold. And after thee shall arise another kingdom inferior to thee; and another third kingdom of brass, which shall bear rule over all the earth. And the fourth kingdom shall be strong as iron, forasmuch as iron breaketh in pieces and subdueth all things; and as iron that crusheth all these, shall it break in pieces and crush. And whereas thou sawest the feet and toes, part of potters' clay, and part of iron, it shall be a divided kingdom; but there shall be in it of the strength of the iron, forasmuch as thou sawest the iron mixed with miry clay. And as the toes of the feet were part of iron, and part of clay, so the kingdom shall be partly strong and partly broken. And whereas thou sawest the iron mixed with miry clay, they shall mingle themselves with the seed of men; but they shall not cleave one to another, even as iron doth not mingle with clay. And in the days of those kings shall the God of heaven set up a kingdom which shall never be destroyed, nor shall the sovereignty thereof be left to another people; but it shall break in pieces and consume all these kingdoms, and it shall stand for ever. Forasmuch as thou sawest that a stone was cut out of the mountain without hands, and that it brake in pieces the iron, the brass, the clay, the silver, and the gold; the great God hath made known to the king what shall come to pass hereafter: and the dream is certain, and the interpretation thereof sure."

Daniel 7:1–14

"In the [first] year of Belshazzar king of Babylon Daniel had a dream and visions of his head upon his bed: then he wrote the dream and told the sum of the matters. Daniel spake and said, I saw in my vision by night, and, behold, the four winds of heaven brake forth upon the great sea. And four great beasts came up from the sea, diverse one from another. The first was like a lion, and had eagle's wings: I beheld till the wings thereof were plucked, and it was lifted up from the earth, and made to stand upon two feet as a man; and a man's heart was given to it. And, behold, another beast, a second, like to a bear; and it was raised up on one side, and three ribs were in its mouth between its teeth: and they said thus unto it, Arise, devour much flesh. After this I beheld, and, lo, another, like a leopard, which had upon its back four wings of a bird; the beast had also four heads; and dominion was given to it. After this I saw in the night-visions, and, behold, a fourth beast, terrible and powerful, and strong exceedingly; and it had great iron teeth; it devoured and brake in pieces, and stamped the residue with its feet: and it was diverse from all the beasts that were before it; and it had ten horns. I considered the horns, and, behold, there came up among them another horn, a little one, before which three of the first horns were plucked up by the roots: and, behold, in this horn were eyes like the eyes of a man, and a mouth speaking great things.

I beheld till thrones were placed, and one that was ancient of days did sit: his raiment was white as snow, and the hair of his head like pure wool; his throne was fiery flames, and the wheels thereof burning fire. A fiery stream issued and came forth from before him: thousands of thousands ministered unto him, and ten thousand times ten thousand stood before him: the judgment was set, and the books were opened. I beheld at that time because of the voice of the great words which the horn spake; I beheld even till the beast was slain, and its body destroyed, and it was given to be burned with fire. And as for the rest of the beasts, their dominion was taken away: yet their lives were prolonged for a season and a time.

I saw in the night-visions, and, behold, there came with the clouds of heaven one like unto a son of man, and he came even to the ancient of days, and they brought him near before him. And there was given him dominion, and glory, and a kingdom, that all the peoples, nations, and languages should serve him: his dominion is an everlasting dominion, which shall not pass away, and his kingdom that which shall not be destroyed.

Shall we just bow together in a word of prayer?

Dear Father, we just want to thank You that You have made available to us all that we need for this evening time and especially for the ministry of Your word. And we together would, Lord, just take that provision by faith. Whether myself speaking or whether the rest of us in hearing, we pray, Lord, that there may be such an anointing upon our time together tonight that we may be given that spirit of wisdom and revelation in the knowledge of Yourself. Lord, let your word come to dwell in us richly we pray. Give us the kind of insight, the kind of understanding that we need for the days in which we're living. Heavenly Father, we just commit ourselves to You now, with thanksgiving, in the name of our Lord Jesus. Amen.

I began to share upon this subject of the relevance of Biblical prophecy. What I had to say was introductory to the rest that I have in my heart. I wish we had the time to deal much more thoroughly with this vital and strategic subject. I would like very much to have talked about some of those basic constituents of Biblical prophecy because it is not all to do just with the future.

The Revelation of God's Eternal Purpose

One of the main aspects or important parts of Biblical prophecy is the revelation of the eternal purpose of God. It is only when we begin to understand what God is driving at, what was the goal He had from the beginning in the creation of the universe and in the creation of man, that we can begin to understand a little more about all the details concerning the nations, concerning the church, concerning Israel, concerning all these other things. They begin to fall into place only when we understand what His eternal and original purpose was. Now, no amount of academic study or intelligence or brainpower will ever bring a man or a woman to an understanding of the eternal purpose of God. It must be revealed. It is the prophetic word of God which has given us an understanding of what that purpose is. That is tremendously important. I wish we had time to spend a whole session on it.

The Matter of Origins

Another aspect of Biblical prophecy, which I consider to be one of the most vital constituents in it, is the matter of origins. All the prophets were continually putting their finger upon the matter of origin. If you have the wrong beginning, you will never end right. In other words, if you begin in Adam, you will never end in God. You have to be got out of Adam and into Christ. You have to have a second birth—a second beginning, a new beginning. If through the death, burial, and resurrection of the Lord Jesus, you have been transferred from Adam and placed in God's Son, you have the right origin. Do you understand? If you have the right origin, your destiny is the glory of God. Everything else falls short of the glory of God. Therefore, it does not matter whether it is Ishmael; if it is Ishmael, he will never inherit. If it is Isaac, born through the promise of God and by the power of God, he inherits. If you belong to Babylon, you can never come to the glory of God. If you have been spiritually born in Jerusalem, then you will inherit the glory of God. So, we could go on. But you see, the prophets are always talking about the matter of origin and it is tremendously important. If we could only see how vital it is, we would understand very much more of the prophetic word. That is why there is so much in it warning us again, and again, and again "make sure of your origins."

The apostle Peter put it very simply, he said, "Make your calling and election sure." In other words, make absolutely certain that your origin is right because origin determines destiny. Now that is something you will find all the way through the Bible; it explains the Bible from Genesis to Revelation.

So, you have these two vital constituents in the word of prophecy. They could not be understood by natural intelligence or brainpower. God revealed them through His prophetic word and in this way, we are given an understanding.

The Outline of World History

Having said that, what I want to talk about this evening is another tremendous aspect of the prophetic word. It is the outline of world history. The Bible gives us an outline of world history. It is the only book in the whole world that has given us an outline of world history from its beginning to its end which has been exact in its accuracy. This means that if it has been so exact in its fulfilment, thus far, we have absolute confidence that what remains yet to be fulfilled will be accurately fulfilled.

Now, God does not give us a detailed history of the nations. It is very interesting when you read the Bible to see what is left out. There are tremendous civilisations and empires that are not even mentioned in the Bible. They are almost passed over, and yet we know that some of these civilisations and empires were some of the greatest in the history of mankind. They are not mentioned because they do not touch the purpose of God. We only have those civilisations and empires mentioned, which in some way or another are involved negatively or positively with the eternal purpose of God. For instance, the only reason the Bible mentions the great Egyptian civilisation is because it had something to do with the unfolding of His purpose for His people. The only reason why we hear of the Babylonian or the Persian or the Greek Empires or the Roman Empire is only because in some way they touch the fulfilment of God's eternal purpose. Everything else is left out. So, we do not have any kind of encyclopaedic outline of all the empires the world has known, of all the civilisations the world has known. What we have is, as it were, history in principle, in particular, where it touches the purpose of God.

Truth Will Ultimately Win

Now, what really is the significance of this outline of world history that we have in the Bible? It is simply this: that truth will ultimately win. Truth will ultimately win. There may be a night of absolute pitch darkness, but in the end the light will win.

The Bible is very interesting because it says God is light and in Him there is no darkness at all. That statement is much more than saying, "God gives light" or "God enlightens people." To say that God *is* light is something far, far more significant and far more important. Jesus said, "I am the truth." If He had said, "I preach the truth," or "I speak the truth," or "I give the truth," that would have been absolutely correct, but it would have been far less than saying, "I *am* the truth."

Now if God is light, and Jesus is the truth, then light and truth must win. There is no question about it at all. Whether the universe is filled with demons, whether there is an Antichrist that rules from end to end of the globe, whether there is a system that enslaves men and women, whether the Bible is finally banned from all places of education, and preaching of the gospel is totally ruled out, it makes no difference to the fact that however dark the night is that might lie ahead, the truth is going to win. That is why God gives us the outline of world history. Furthermore, He is not afraid to bring before our vision pictures of very great savagery and bestiality. God does not hide it all behind a curtain.

He brings it all before our eyes and says, "Now listen, if you have no faith you will fear, but if you have the eyes of faith, you will see right the way through to the ultimate victory of the Lamb." No matter what the darkness, no matter what the power and authority of evil, no matter what is done physically to those who belong to God, in the end truth must win.

Now of course, the apostle John put it very simply in I John 4:4, he said this, speaking about the Antichrist and so on, he said, "Ye are of God, my little children, and have overcome them: because greater is He that is in you than he that is in the world." Now, I find this quite tremendous. The child of God has no need to fear nuclear war. They can blow your body to pieces but the One who is in you is greater than he that is in the world, and He can put back your body in a single moment of time. After all, does it matter if we go in a big bang, or if we die on a bed of sickness? Our bodies are going to go back to dust anyway, and one day there is going to be a miracle of resurrection in which all the atoms that have made up your body are regathered together, and you are given a resurrection body, a redemption body. It is a miracle! Truth will win!

Jesus said this wonderful thing about martyrdom, He said, "This will happen to you, and this will happen to you, and this will happen to you, but do not fear for not one hair of your head will perish". Now, I think that is wonderful, He did not just say, "Do not worry. You will have a whole being in the end." He went to these hairs which drop out every day and said, "Not one hair of your head will perish." Not *one* hair of your head will perish. I imagine even the bald will get back a head full of hair in the end. Truth will win because truth is Jesus. Light will win because

God is light. If He has gone to so much trouble to redeem you, spirit, soul, and body, if you walk with Him and if you trust Him, and if you do His will, you will not suffer, ultimately. In the end, you will be there in glory with Him, not one hair of your head will be lost.

Now, I say that is quite tremendous. We have no need to fear nuclear war, some people are so frightened to death of it that is why they get so worked up in an escapist way concerning the rapture. They think, "Ooh, ooh, we must have a rapture. We cannot face a war. We have got to go before and ..." it is nonsense! Just supposing the Lord has so ordered it that we have another world war. Are you going to lose your faith because you have all along thought, "No, no, no, no! We are never going to have anything like that. We are going to go before." Praise God if we all go before! But if we must go through another world war, why should we fear? Greater is He that is in us than he that is in the world. We have no need to fear. Why should we fear Antichrist? Let him come. Let him do everything he wants to do. He will come and he will do everything that he wants to do. Why? Because it says God will allow him to speak these great words of blasphemy and to do every single thing that he wants to do. But he has a predestined time of appearing, and thank God, a predestined time for finishing. His appearance, and his end, are foreordained by God.

It is most beautifully put in Thessalonians where it says, "And the Lord Jesus will slay him with the breath of His mouth and by the brightness of His appearing" II Thessalonians 2:8. How simple. It will not seem too good when the Antichrist is here and if, in the will of God, we should live through at least the first part of his appearing it will not seem so simple then. It will seem that he will have a cast iron system and a power that is unparalleled in the history of mankind. But oh, how marvellous it is that truth is going to win! All the Lord Jesus has to do is appear and breathe on him and he will shrivel in an instant. Thank God for that!

"Greater is He that is in you than he that is in the world," (1 John 4:4). The most priceless thing in the whole world is to know the indwelling of the Lord Jesus. What can you compare with a human being? Especially some of us, decaying, grotty, not very beautiful, slowly decomposing, and yet we have within us the Son of God. The Son of God is in us! Dwelling in our mortal bodies! Able to quicken them! How tremendous that is! Why, you could have all the gold in the gold mines of South Africa and the Soviet Union and yet, it pales into insignificance compared with the indwelling of the Lord Jesus. I could have so many diamonds that I could be smothered with them, and, yet, I am the poorest man in the history of the world if I do not have the Lord Jesus living within my mortal body. Diamonds, or platinum, or gold, or silver—they are worth nothing compared with the indwelling of the Lord Jesus. What a privilege it is, as human beings, to have received the Son of God into our hearts and into our beings and into our lives to have been joined into a union with God in Christ! We sometimes murmur and complain and rebel and devalue our salvation, yet we are the recipients of the greatest treasure that this world knows—the fathomless, unsearchable riches of the Lord Jesus.

"Greater is He that is in you than he that is in the world" (1 John 4:4). I remind myself continually, though it is a mystery, that the devil is a created being. God created him. Why, I do not know. One day I shall ask and maybe we shall get an answer. But it comforts me to know that the devil is not infinite. He is not like God without beginning or end. He is a created, finite being, with the greatest intelligence in the universe and great power and authority, but he is a created being. In me, is an uncreated being, thank God for that! In me, and in you is the Son of God—God the Son.

"Greater is He that is in you than he that is in the world." Does it not blow your mind, the very thought of it? My dear friend, when you go back to your room, go to the mirror. Have a look and say to yourself, "Look, can you believe it? In that body lives the Son of God. In me! Not a created spirit, not some principality or power, but the Son of God Himself lives within me!" "Greater is He that is in you than he that is in the world!" We have no need to fear nuclear war. Why should we? We have no need to fear the Antichrist. Why should we? His coming is predestined, his power is predestined, his duration of time is predestined, and thank God, his end is predestined. Why should we fear? It is rather like going to the dentist without anaesthetic—a sharp pain and it is all over. We can endure these things if we see beyond to the glory that is to be, to the kingdom of God, which is forever. Truth will win because truth is God.

Now I say that this is very satisfying. We have no reason to fear these things for the satisfying reason that we are on the winning side! I think it is always good to be on the winning side. I do not know how you feel, but I think it is a tremendous thing to be on the winning side. I thank God that He took me out of the losing side and put me on the winning side! Adam's is the losing side. Satan's is the losing side. Christ's is the winning side. God is the winning side. Oh, I thank God, He delivered me from the power of darkness and transferred me into the kingdom of the Son of His love. We are on the winning side. So, we should encourage ourselves.

"Greater is He that is in us than he that is in the world." Now the problem is that he that is in the world is sometimes a good deal more manifest than He that is in us. We so often see the circumstances and feel the influence of he that is in the world. When he does this war dance around us it sometimes seems that he has all the power and all the authority and that he is there forever. But it is not true. That is why we have the outline of world history. It is as if God is saying, "I know how the enemy is going to work on you my dear children. I know that he will bring you to a place of discouragement, of despair, of despondency where perhaps you will be tempted to throw away your so great confidence and therefore, I have given you an outline of world history. I have not hidden from your gaze any of the dark things, or the evil things, or the savagery, or the wickedness, or the triumph of darkness. I have depicted it all as it will come to pass, so that when these things are fulfilled you do not lose faith or heart, but you see through it to the ultimate victory of the Lord Jesus." Now you can understand why "the word of prophecy is a lamp in a dark and squalid place to which we should give heed".

The Times of the Gentiles

Now, it was to Daniel that God gave this understanding of what we call the times of the Gentiles. Daniel was born of nobility. In fact, we have an ancient Jewish tradition, which I imagine is probably true, that Daniel was born of the royal house of David. Certainly, Daniel was of aristocratic birth and it was precisely because of his noble birth that he was deported by Nebuchadnezzar in 606 BC, when all those of good birth and upper, sort of, good pedigree, were taken away to Babylon. They were there investigated and examined and the very choicest of them were made eunuchs. Daniel was amongst them. For three years he went through the training program and then entered into royal service. Now, the interesting thing is this: that from the very beginning, when he was a teenager, Daniel, who knew the Lord, determined not to compromise on one single issue. It must have been a very great temptation to him to have compromised so as to win favour. Maybe his argument might have gone, "Well, it does not matter very much if I have to eat things that are not right and which are against the Levitical law and do this, and do that, and the other. After all, it is more important to remain alive, and later on perhaps times will be better and then I can start to go back to this when I have greater favour with the authorities." But not Daniel. From the very beginning, he purposed not to defile himself in any single way and God brought him from one influential position to another, right through the successive reigns of Babylonian kings and Persian kings, until, in the end, this Jewish boy became the supreme administrator of the whole Persian Empire. First, he became one of the committee of three that ran the whole nation under the king and finally he became the first of the three in the greatest empire the world had ever known.

It was to this man that God gave an understanding of world history. He revealed to him the times of the Gentiles. Now it is the Lord Jesus who used this term: "the times of the Gentiles" as it is recorded in the gospel of Luke and chapter 21:24. "And they," that is the Jewish people, "shall fall by the edge of the sword and shall be led captive into all the nations and Jerusalem shall be trodden down of the Gentiles until the times of the Gentiles be fulfilled."

We must not confuse, at least in my estimation, this phrase, this term, "the times of the Gentiles," with the apostle Paul's term in Romans 11:25, "the fulness of the Gentiles." Some people think that the times of the Gentiles and the fulness of the Gentiles are the same thing. But the fulness of the Gentiles is a term meaning the full number of the Gentiles, of the elect people of God amongst the Gentiles. The times of the Gentiles refer to something else. Now, I think that is quite important and I just want to underline it and go straight on.

I read to you two chapters in Daniel. (I hope what I have got to say is not too complex; it is a complex subject.) In the first, when Daniel was in his 20s, a dream-vision was given, not to Daniel, but to the Emperor, King Nebuchadnezzar. Finally, God gave to Daniel the interpretation of that dream. Do you remember the dream? Nebuchadnezzar saw a huge colossus, a huge idol, a huge image of a human being. Its head was gold, its chest and arms were silver, its belly and thighs were bronze, its legs were iron, and its feet baked clay and iron mixed together, two materials that do not fuse. Then, as he watched, suddenly, a stone was cut—not humanly, without hands—out of a mountain of rock and was sent hurtling towards the statue. It did not hit the head, nor the chest, nor the thighs, nor even the legs. It hit the feet. In that moment, the whole great 90 ft. high statue collapsed into a heap. It was shattered beyond repair. Then as the king watched, he saw this stone, this rock which had been cut out of a mountain, but not with human hands, grow, and grow, and grow, and grow, until it filled the whole earth.

To Daniel was given the understanding. He said, "You, O king Nebuchadnezzar, are the head of gold." That is, this outline of history, these times of the Gentiles begin with the Babylonian Empire, and in particular with king Nebuchadnezzar, the greatest of the Babylonian kings. "After you, there shall come another empire which is inferior ..." What followed was the Persian Empire—dramatically, suddenly, overnight. We know from the Bible, don't we, because Daniel was part of it all. Do you remember? In that great feast the hand wrote on the wall and Daniel said to the last Babylonian king, Belshazzar, "You have been weighed in the balances and found wanting. This night the kingdom will be taken from you and given to another" (Daniel 5:27). In that night, the Persian army dammed up one of the great canals of Babylon and came through the river gate and took the whole city. The whole Babylonian Empire disappeared, never to reappear again. So, the next part of the statue, the silver chest and arms, is Persia. The greatest empire from the human point of view that the world had seen to that time, for it stretched nearly all the way to India. Then said Daniel, "After this empire there will arise another empire of bronze ...," What followed the Persian Empire? The Greek, the Hellenic, which stretched all the way from Greece in Europe to northern India ... After that, there will be another kingdom, diverse and strong, that will crush everything to pieces." We know that the fourth empire was Rome.

Now, you wonder, "Well, is that all there is to world history?" No, because if we go on, we find that the whole thing continues right down to modern times. Modern civilisation is a conglomerate of Babylonian, Persian, Greek, and Roman things with a little bit of mixture of Biblical things as well. That is modern civilisation, and it is a very interesting fact that we are now witnessing the process by which our present civilisation is returning to its pagan origins, and throwing overboard everything that has come from the Jewish/Christian side. We are in this very process at the present time.

Daniel's Dream-Vision

Now, it is a very interesting thing that in Daniel chapter 7, Daniel records a dream-vision that was given to him. This time it is not an image or a colossus. (I hope you can follow me.) This time it is four savage beasts. The first was a lion, the second was a bear, the third was a leopard, and the fourth was a creature that Daniel had never seen before, which he described as "exceedingly diverse and strong and fierce" (Daniel 7:7). Four beasts. Now, the lion corresponds to the head of gold, the bear corresponds to the chest and arms of silver, the leopard corresponds to the belly and thighs of bronze, and the diverse beast, the fourth one corresponds to the legs. There are some people who say that it does not, but I will leave that to another time. They say that it does not end with Rome, but ends with the Greek Empire; or some of them say that it will be a revival of the Babylonian Empire in the last days. I am not at all convinced for the simple reason that the Scripture says that in the days of those kings, God will set up a kingdom which shall never be destroyed. When did the Lord Jesus appear on the earth? Not in the Greek Empire, not in the

Persian Empire, not in the Babylonian Empire, but in the Roman era. We have witnessed the whole of that right down to the present day. We are the product of that Roman civilisation. I do hope I am making this at least a little clear. I hope you will not be more confused at the end of this than when we began.

John's Vision

In Revelation chapter 13 we have a most remarkable thing. There, suddenly, John sees coming up out of the sea—just as Daniel saw the winds breaking from four quarters onto the sea and churning it up into a great sort of storm, a hurricane force storm—John sees coming out of the sea, the restless sea, a great beast and it is a composite beast. Lion, bear, leopard, and that last creature all mixed up into one. In other words, it is as if modern civilisation is the conglomerate of Babylonian, Persian, Greek, and Roman ideals and philosophy. It is exactly the same if you look very carefully.

What is this all about?

Now maybe you begin to wonder, oh dear, what is all this about? If we had time, we could talk about all the details of this, for they are fascinating. So accurate was Daniel's prophetic insight that liberal, modernist, Bible scholars have said it could not possibly have been Daniel who foretold all this. No one could describe empires a century or two before they came to pass in such accurate detail. These are men who normally would like to discredit it all, so what they say is, "This is such a remarkably accurate record of the Greek period in particular, that it must have been written afterwards in the guise of prophecy." At least everyone admits it is accurate. It is a question of whether it was written up after the event or predicted before the event. Well, I think you know. We can say, we believe that God is able to do anything. He is well able to speak of Cyrus, 200 years before he appears. Why can't He? He is well able to speak of the Greek Empire and Alexander the Great, and then after his whirlwind victories the whole empire breaking up into four kingdoms, then two of them becoming the principal ones—the South centred on Egypt, the North centred on Syria and the battles between the two. Then this extraordinary king called Antiochus IV Epiphanes, who is the original antichrist of the Bible.

This man was a most remarkable man. I will not spend too much time upon him, except to say this: that you have in these different visions a little horn mentioned, or a contemptible person mentioned, or a king of the north mentioned, and they are all the same person. Although they refer to different times in history, they are all predictive of a man who is going to come at the end of the age, in our generation I believe, a man of tremendous culture and sophistication, a man who believes in democratic principles, who will sweep the whole world after him and will produce a system in which war and terrorism will be banned. A new kind of morality and a new pattern for living will be initiated or introduced. This man is called in the New Testament, the man of sin, or the Antichrist.

Now it is not my purpose to say too much about him now. All I want to say is this: we have an outline of world history here, which if we only had the time, we could go into it in detail and show you how amazingly accurate it has been. What I find so interesting is this: we have here a revelation of what we call the times of the Gentiles, which began with King Nebuchadnezzar. Have they ended? What are the times of the Gentiles? Why is it called the times of the Gentiles? Because it speaks of the subjugation of the Jewish people. It was called the times of the Gentiles because the Jewish people were not sovereign but subservient. Those times began with Nebuchadnezzar, with certain exceptions for up to, in one instance, almost 100 years, and have lasted all the way through the Roman time and right the way through the last 2000 years right into this generation.

Now listen to me very carefully. If these times of the Gentiles mean the subjugation of the Jewish people, that is, their being brought under the sovereignty of Gentile superpowers or Gentile nations, then surely the emergence of a sovereign Jewish state ought to spell the end of those times. On the 14th of May 1948, a sovereign Jewish state appeared amongst the nations of the world, and therefore, we can say that the times of the Gentiles have ended. Now is that correct or is it incorrect? Because there are those who say, "No, no that is not so. The times of the Gentiles means the times of unbelievers and this means that the unbelieving peoples and nations will trample down Jerusalem until Jesus comes again.

Now just hang on. Look at this word again in Luke 21:23–24. This is what Jesus says, "Woe unto them that are with child and to them that give suck in those days for there shall be great distress upon the land ..." What land? The land of Israel. "... and wrath unto this people ..." Which people? The Jewish people. "... and they shall fall by the edge of the sword." Which people will fall by the edge of the sword? The Jewish people, "... and they shall be led captive into all the nations ..." That happened in 70 AD. "... and Jerusalem shall be trodden down of the Gentiles until the times of the Gentiles be fulfilled." In other words, the Lord Jesus was speaking to the Jewish people about their national territory, about their national capital, and about their statehood. All these things would disappear until the times of the Gentiles be fulfilled.

What does that mean? It means this, that on the 14th of May 1948, God began to tie up something that He first revealed to His servant Daniel 2,600 years ago. The times of the Gentiles were fulfilled. But I have some more evidence if I can persuade you, or at least put before you so that you can consider it. "Jerusalem shall be trodden down of the Gentiles until the times of the Gentiles be fulfilled." Never at any time in the last 2,000 years has Jerusalem been under the sovereign government of Jews, except for a few months in 135 AD in the *Bar Kokhba* rebellion. That is the only time. In all the last 2,000 years, Jerusalem has been under the heel of Gentile nations of one kind or another up until June 6th, 1967 when in a lightning move, the Israeli defence forces retook the old city of Jerusalem, reunited it with west Jerusalem and on the 30th of July 1980, by act of Knesset, it was proclaimed the eternal and indivisible capital of the Jewish people. Now listen to the actual words of the act of Parliament, the Jewish Parliament, "It is proclaimed the indivisible and eternal capital of the Jewish people."

"Jerusalem shall be trodden down of the Gentiles until the times of the Gentiles be fulfilled." What has happened? First, there has been the emergence in 1948 of a sovereign Jewish state, and now Jerusalem has been retaken to become the capital of that sovereign Jewish state. The times of the Gentiles are over! Then what time are we in? Into what have we been led as the people of God? We have been introduced into that phase, if I am right, and I may be wrong, but if I am right (and I think I am right) we have been led into what is called in the Scripture, "the last days," or "the end times," or I like it much more, "the threshold of the Messiah's coming." Jesus said, "When you see these things coming to pass know you that He is nigh, even at the door!" Matthew 24:33. You can hear His footstep on the threshold of the door when you see these things beginning to come to pass. How exciting!

People get all frightened and say, "Oh dear, dear, dear! Are we going to see persecution? Are we going to suffer the Antichrist? Is there going to be another world war?" Well, my dear friends, it is what you look at. Of course, if you want nuclear war, you can have it. If you want the Antichrist, you can have him. If you want persecution, you may well have to suffer it. But my dear friends, that is not the point. The point is this: we are on the threshold of the Messiah's coming! That is exciting, at least it is for me! I hope it is for you.

Do you see how this word of prophecy is a lamp shining in a dark and squalid place to which we do well to give heed? II Peter 1:19. What would we do without this word of prophecy? It is vitally important that the people of God should at least know where they are in world history. We are not in the Babylonian era. We are not in the Persian era. We are not in the Greek era. We are not even, in one sense, in the Roman era, thank God. We are in the last days. We have passed out of the times of the Gentiles and into the last days of the age. Now, I do not know how long they will last, some people say a generation. I personally am not very much with it because if it is a generation from 1948, we can date the coming of the Lord, can't we? Some will say, "Oh no, no, no, no, He is going to come before then." Well then, we can date it even more clearly, can't we—sometime between now and 1988 He is going to come. I am not very sure about this.

What I know and it thrills my heart, and my spirit starts to jump and leap as I think: well, here we are in a last period, however long it lasts, we have got a work to do as the people of God! We have got to see the bride prepared. We have got to see the issues in our lives settled. We have got to hold forth the word of life to dying multitudes all around us. We have no time to lose! We have passed irrevocably, irreversibly out of the times of the Gentiles, thank God, into the last days. Are you ready?

Are you ready? Supposing He came tonight, are you ready? Or would you like Him to give you another week? I am not being funny; would you like Him to give you another week so that you could get things settled? In other words, you are not ready. There are people you should write letters to, phone calls you should make, difficulties that need to be overcome, forgiveness sought, humbling made. I know many people who would say, "Oh please, please, do not let Him come tonight. I have got a few things I need to do."

Dear people of God, you will not know when He comes. He will come like a thief. It is time to get ready. There is no time like today! So, we need to begin to get ready. Some of you say, "Oh, could you not just give me a little more time? I want to grow more in the Lord." My dear child of God, just you settle the issues in your heart with the Lord, and be obedient to Him, and He will make you grow very quickly if necessary. Normally, God must give time to you that you might grow, but there are times when there is the right spirit, when God can put you, as it were, if I may so speak, into a pressure cooker and get you more quickly done than otherwise. You may not like the pressure cooker spiritually, but God can do it if you are ready and willing.

The First Lesson from this Prophetic Word

Now, dear people of God what are the lessons from this prophetic word? I find it a tremendous comfort to myself to know that God is working out His purpose. From the beginning He has been working everything according to His purpose. Well, I find that very exciting! I think to myself, supposing I had lived in the days of Nebuchadnezzar before he was converted. I think I might have been very afraid. When he set up that great 90-foot image and said, "Everyone is to bow down and worship." The power of the man! He only had to flick a finger and someone's head came off! I would have said, "Oh! What am I to do now? He has supreme authority." It may not have been quite so easy to realise God was behind Nebuchadnezzar. In all his wickedness, in all his unbelief, God was behind him. He had his beginning, and he had his end.

If I had lived in the time of Antiochus IV when he defiled the temple, I would have been really afraid, for he changed all the laws. He banned the Sabbath. He said there could be no more circumcision. He made the Jews eat non-kosher food. He sacrificed a pig on the brazen altar in the temple and then went into the Holy of Holies with the blood of a pig and sprinkled it in the Holy of Holies! He caused immoral rites and orgies to be held within the temple precincts. He set up a statue of himself upon the brazen altar and took the name "Epiphanies, Outshining of God," because he believed that he was a manifestation of God in the flesh. He caused the blood of godly people to flow from end to end of the country for seven years. If I had lived in the time of Antiochus, I might have feared and wondered, "What can I do? Shall I compromise to save my skin?" But Antiochus had a beginning and Antiochus had an end. I find that a tremendous comfort.

All the tyrants of world history, strangely enough, have only come to the zenith of their power by the allowance and permission and authority of God. This means that every empire that ever has come to rule and reign has come by God's ordering and both its rise and its fall have been ordained. It is the same with all the ideologies. "Oh," you say, "You cannot say that surely. Do you mean to tell me that Marxism has been ordained by God?" Yes, I do. The rise of Marxism was within the sovereignty of God. Its rise to power, the duration of its time, and its fall are all ordained by God. It does not matter whether it is the Babylonian Empire, or the Persian Empire, or the Greek Empire, or the Roman Empire. It does not matter whether it is the Holy Roman Empire, or whether it is the British Empire, or whether it is the Austro-Hungarian Empire, or the Chinese Empire, or whether the Russian Empire, they all came to their power and all came to their end. It does not matter whether it is the superpowers of the present era. The United States is at present at the zenith of its power. God has ordained its beginning, its rise to power, the duration of its time, and its fall. God has ordained the rise of the Soviet Union, and its rise to power, the duration of its time, and its fall. Marxism, Capitalism, both of them are under the sovereign hand of God. He is not, as it were, the Master of them, or in some way the Producer of them, but He is the one who works out His purpose through them all!

God's Kingdom is Forever
I remember an old Danish sister that some of us knew very well, who was one of the most remarkable women I think that Denmark produced as far as the house of God is concerned. I had a friend who went to her when the Nazis invaded Denmark in 1940. As the air raid sirens wailed, and as these German bombers dived in, dive bombing a nearby town, and as others came along and machine-gunned people in the lanes and in the fields, there she was out in the garden with a little spade planting petunias. Her friend, who dashed in through the gate, saw her on her knees planting away and singing quietly to herself and said, "Sophia, Sophia, you must go in! The Germans are bombing!" She looked up, and she said, "The Germans will come, and the Germans will go. Only God is forever," and went on planting her petunias.

You know, we must learn some of these lessons. God is working out His purpose. Maybe you would have preferred to have been in a period of peace rather than a period of war. It seems rather sad from the vantage point of time that some of us must spend our whole little life, say, under the heel of a Marxist tyrant. But whether it is Stalin, or whether it is Mao, or whoever it is, they come and they go, but the kingdom of God is forever. These other kingdoms, God uses and discards; His kingdom is forever. That is the first lesson.

The Second Lesson from this Prophetic Word

The second lesson that I find of tremendous help is this: do you notice that when God reveals the times of the Gentiles, He reveals it in terms of an idol? A huge colossus or image of a man? Do you think it is not interesting that in the very next chapter, Nebuchadnezzar set up such an image, 90-feet high and had all the band come out and play? Do you remember, and whenever the band played everyone had to prostrate themselves before this image? We are not told that that image was the image he saw, but the association seems clear.

The Deification of Man

Now, what am I trying to say in this? I am saying precisely this: human history is the deification of man. It is a process of self-worship. If you look at world history, man has risen to his greatest heights driven by self-worship, and he has gone down to the greatest depths of depravity for the same reason. This is why, when we hear of this beast coming out of the sea in the last book of the Bible, we are given a number 666—the number of man. It says again and again the dragon will cause all people to worship the beast. Then it says that the false prophet will come and will set up an image and cause all the nations to worship that image of the beast. Is it not interesting, history repeating itself in the final analysis? I find that very interesting. Human history is an image—very beautiful at times, very sophisticated, very refined, but an image that man worships.

Now here is something else also I find very interesting: a statue is immobile. It has no heart. All these great ideologies, whatever they are through human history, they have appeared so magnificent, but they are lifeless. Man is drawn into them like cogs in a machine. His individuality, his originality is destroyed. We have seen in our own generation such great things. Take some of the tenants of Marxism. They are so socially just, so magnificent in concept and yet it is a huge monolith without a heart that grinds human beings into nothing. An idol. I find that very interesting.

Human History in the Picture of Savage Beasts

May I go on to another lesson which I find also very interesting? This same picture of human history is given to us in another way, only this time in the picture of savage beasts, so that suddenly we see behind the facade, the sophisticated facade of the image, what it really is: savagery. I do not know whether I need to go through history to talk about savagery. You would have thought that man after these thousands of years of existence would have finally learnt his lesson, but my dear friends, the 20th century has been as savage as any other single era of human history. Do you know how many people died in two world wars alone? The 1914–1918 war and the 1939–1945 war? Fifty-five million people died in those two wars; fifty-five *million* people died. Twenty million died in concentration camps alone in the Far East and in Europe. Savagery.

Four Twentieth Century Examples

I can give four instances taken from this century that I think are like a capsule form. These will give you an understanding of this picture of world history as four savage, wild beasts—the cruelty, the inhumanity, the bestiality of man without God.

The Armenian Genocide

The first example is in 1915—1918, the genocide of the Armenian people. The Armenian people are amongst the most artistic and gifted of all the peoples on the face of the earth. But for no other reason than that they were Armenian and Christians, the Turkish Muslims fell upon them and murdered 1,400,000 at least. In forced marches, men, women, children, and babes in arms were butchered mercilessly. That is the 20th century.

The Holocaust

My second example is much nearer to us, 1940—1944, four years in which six million Jews, men, women, children, babes in arms were butchered in the most horrifying circumstances. All that the modern world could conceive were used in that—gas ovens to simply liquidate people, nor were the remains even dumped. The teeth were taken out, the gold was extracted and melted into gold bars, the hair was shaved off to use for mattresses, even the skin was used in some cases for lampshades, the flesh was melted down for soap, and the bones were ground into powder for fertiliser. This is not 2000 years ago. It is not 3000 years ago, the Babylonian wickedness, or the Assyrian cruelty, or the Roman hardness. This is the middle of the 20th century and one of the most cultured peoples in the whole of Europe, the German people, when they became demonised through Nazism. I have friends who witnessed one month old babes tossed into the air and caught on bayonets as they came down, and others who saw little children thrown alive into the furnaces. Surgery was performed upon human beings without anaesthetic, in which living organs were removed from them without even anaesthetic.

Can you believe that in your generation such things could happen? World history depicted as savage wild beasts.

Soviet Union Labour Camps

I will give you another example. In the years of the rise of the Soviet Union, for no other reason than for political dissidence, 15 million people have died in forced labour camps, in the most inhuman and bestial circumstances. Today, thank God, there are not so many concentration camps in the Soviet Union, but you know the new thing is to send people to hospitals where they are injected with a brain drug which destroys their ability to think. This is the 1970s, the 1980s! Wild, savage beasts.

Cambodian Genocide

My last example is right near to hand. It is the Cambodian tragedy, when the Khmer Rouge took over that little beautiful land and murdered two million people in a bloodbath of unparalleled savagery.[1] Why? Because they wanted to destroy a whole class of people that radical Marxism might take root. People in hospitals were taken out of hospitals in a de-urbanisation program in which whole towns and cities were driven into the fields and people who just had surgery all the things were disconnected and as they were taken out, they died.

Now, my dear friends, you may not like to hear such things as these, these are not the cosy, comforting little things that so often Christians are content to listen to. These are the dark, savage, evil, but realistic things of this world. This is why when God speaks of the times of the Gentiles of world history, He depicts it

1 1975—1979

first in the form of an image, an idol, and covetousness, says the Bible, which is idolatry. It is human greed that lies at the root of all this self-worship and self-gratification. However, it is not just a beautiful idol. Behind the idol is the savagery of wild animals, men and women without God, brute beasts.

Dear friends, we have Daniel to thank for this revelation concerning world history. Shall I tell you something? I am undisguisedly thankful it is coming to an end. It may have beautiful architecture, and beautiful music, and beautiful literature, but behind its facade of sophistication and refinement and education, are savage beasts.

The Lamb is Forever

Thank God there is an end to it all! When it ends then all things will be made new and that is the last lesson I want to leave with you. The message of the times of the Gentiles of this outline of world history is not all bestiality and cruelty and wickedness. The wickedness and cruelty of the beast is for a time only. The grace and the glory of the Lamb is forever. It is a supreme point of divine inspiration that it is a lamb that is seen in the throne of God. Could there be anything more different to a beast than a lamb? A little lamb. There could be nothing more different. On one side, dragons, serpents, beasts, false prophets, Babylon with all its glory and splendour and avarice; and on the other side, a little lamb as if had been slain. But the message of Daniel is that this one who was like to a son of man, who came to the Ancient of Days, into His hands were given glory and honour and dominion and a kingdom that shall not pass away.

I am very thankful for the Bible. I am thankful it does not hide from me the real facts concerning the nations and concerning world history. I am even more thrilled that the character of the one who is King of kings and Lord of lords is not a beast, but a lamb. In His hand, authority and power are safe. Oh, dear people of God, we are meant to be followers of the Lamb. We are those who are meant to follow the Lamb whithersoever He goes.

So dear people, we conclude here for now. I hope you do not find it too depressing and too dark to have talked about these times of the Gentiles. Let me say it once again: they have ended! We have before us the last, darkest part of the night. Thank God, I personally do not believe we shall have to endure too much of it. There are those who believe we shall have to endure the whole of it. I will not argue with you. I will love you and I hope you will love me too. If we go through this darkest part of the night to the end, please support me and help me, it will be a bit of a shock. But this I can tell you, that the grace and the power of God will be sufficient for whatever we have to face. These times of the Gentiles are over, thank God! Now we are in the last phase for however long it lasts. Are you ready? Here is the word of prophecy which is a lamp shining in a dark place whereunto you and I do well to take heed until the day dawn, and the Daystar arise in our hearts.

3.
God's Divine Time Clock

1 Thessalonians 5:1–11

But concerning the times and the seasons, brethren, ye have no need that aught be written unto you. For yourselves know perfectly that the day of the Lord so cometh as a thief in the night. When they are saying, Peace and safety, then sudden destruction cometh upon them, as travail upon a woman with child; and they shall in no wise escape. But ye, brethren, are not in darkness, that that day should overtake you as a thief: for ye are all sons of light, and sons of the day: we are not of the night, nor of darkness; so then let us not sleep, as do the rest, but let us watch and be sober. For they that sleep sleep in the night; and they that are drunken are drunken in the night. But let us, since we are of the day, be sober, putting on the breastplate of faith and love; and for a helmet, the hope of salvation. For God appointed us not unto wrath, but unto the obtaining of salvation through our Lord Jesus Christ, who died for us, that, whether we wake or sleep, we should live together with him. *Wherefore exhort one another, and build each other up, even as also ye do.*

Mark 13:28–37
Now from the fig tree learn her parable: when her branch is now become tender, and putteth forth its leaves, ye know that the summer is nigh; even so ye also, when ye see these things coming to pass, know ye that he is nigh, even at the doors. Verily I say unto you, This generation shall not pass away, until all these things be accomplished. Heaven and earth shall pass away: but my words shall not pass away. But of that day or that hour knoweth no one, not even the angels in heaven, neither the Son, but the Father.

Take ye heed, watch and pray: for ye know not when the time is. It is as when a man, sojourning in another country, having left his house, and given authority to his servants, to each one his work, commanded also the porter to watch. Watch therefore: for ye know not when the lord of the house cometh, whether at even, or at midnight, or at cockcrowing, or in the morning; lest coming suddenly he find you sleeping. And what I say unto you I say unto all, Watch.

Shall we bow together in the word of prayer?

Heavenly Father, we want to thank You this morning that we are here in Your presence, and we thank You for all that is ours in the Lord Jesus and thank You that You have a design and a plan for this day. We praise You for Your power and ability to fulfil that design. Father, none of us want to get in Your way. We want just to be in Your hand for the fulfilment of that plan. For this morning, we commit ourselves to You Lord. Will You fill this time with Your anointing so that, Lord, we really do hear You and Your Word comes not just into our heads but into our hearts. That something may happen within our lives, Lord, that will, as it were, bring us face-to-face with realities, and enable us to understand the time that we are living in and the urgency of the hour. We ask all this with thanksgiving in the name of our Lord Jesus. Amen.

In this passage in 1 Thessalonians 5, the apostle Paul by the Holy Spirit says in verse 4, "But ye, brethren, are not in darkness that that day should overtake you as a thief." Would to God that every child of God was really alive to the hour in which we are now living. However, it is a sad fact that a large number of the Lord's people, including those who have some knowledge of prophecy, are asleep.

Like A Thief

I remember years ago an incident that has always remained in my mind and memory. I was only in the very beginning of my teens; I think I was about 12 years of age. My mother and stepfather were away, and we were in the tender mercies of an aunt. Suddenly at about two o'clock in the night, she burst into my room and said, "Lance! Lance! Get up quickly for the whole avenue is filled with police cars and police dogs! Someone must be burgled!" So, leaping out of bed, I followed her across the landing into the big front bedroom, and across the bedroom to the window. There my sister was already hanging out of the window watching all the movements of cars purring almost silently up and down, black limousines and what we call in Britain "Black Marias." (Those are the police vans they use to lock up whoever they catch.) Policeman were going in and out of the gardens with torches and great Alsatian dogs, (I think here you call them German Shepherd dogs) very quietly, with just little whispers, so we couldn't hear what was going on. My aunt was hanging out the window with my sister and they were both saying, "I wonder who it is?" My aunt would say, "I'm sure it's so-and-so. Serves him right!"

Then there was somebody else, "No, no, no," my sister said, "I think it's so-and-so. I don't think it's so-and-so because they've been in and out of there three times and they haven't got anyone."

So, they would watch, and then all of a sudden after about 25 minutes, my aunt said, "Oh, I am thirsty. I think I'll go downstairs and make myself a coffee," so she trotted off down the stairs. Well, in a few moments we heard a shriek that could raise the dead in the parish graveyard two miles across the River Thames on the other side! She was up on that landing faster than one of your rockets takes off from Cape Canaveral. Shaking like a leaf, white as snow, she stood on the landing and said, "He's in *our* kitchen!"

So, we both gawked at her and said, "What? The thief is in *our* kitchen?!"

"Yes," she said, "he was sitting at the kitchen table eating one of your mother's blancmanges! Really!" She said, "When I went in, he said, 'Good evening, Madam.'" She did not wait to pass the time of day or night with him, but *fled* upstairs as fast as possible. Of course, we were told later by the police that they never did get him on that occasion. He was a famous cat burglar and he had been in 13 houses that night, one after another in this whole area. He of course went out the way he came in having had his blancmange, he didn't take anything else and went off into the night. But the thing that always tickled my perverted sense of humour was that we were trying to find where and to what neighbour the thief had made or paid a visit, and he was sitting in *our own kitchen*!

I have often wondered whether that's exactly what will happen to many, many Christians when the Lord comes. They are so *busy* thinking, "So-and-so should wake up, that group should hear this, that group should hear that." However, they *themselves* are unaware that the thief might be in their own kitchen.

"You brethren are not in darkness that that day should overtake you as a thief." The Lord has given so many warnings to his disciples: "Take heed, watch and pray, and what I say to you I say to all, watch". If our Lord was so *emphatic* in this matter, there must be a very real possibility of some kind of loss if we do not take heed to His advice. If we are so stupid as to believe that we are ready, when maybe we are not ready and that, "Everyone else needs to get ready, except myself," we could be found out when the Lord comes.

Sleep and Drunkenness

It is very interesting what the apostle Paul says here in verses 6 and 7, "... so then let us not sleep, as do the rest, but let us watch and be sober. For they that sleep, sleep in the night: and they that are drunken are drunken in the night." Now sleep (which just at present I am not having too great an experience of) but sleep is a state of inertia. Is that not right? Immobility, you are horizontal. Now this doesn't mean, of course, you don't move around a bit and so on, but basically sleep is a state of inertia. I think many Christians are in this state. Inertia. They are not moving; they haven't moved for years. Of course, up here in their minds they can get more but here in their hearts nothing happens. They are in a state of inertia. Their kind of Christian service is a sleep-walking routine. It is quite automatic. It is something that they don't have to think about, it doesn't cost them too much. It is a routine.

What is drunkenness? Drunkenness is a form of escapism. When a person takes to drink, they are running away from something. Normally, they are running away from their circumstances, or from relationships, or from some complex problem they have inherited in their own temperament, and they cannot face up to it. They take to drink and somehow try to put themselves into a position where they don't know. Drunkenness.

Now it is a tragedy, but it is possible to use even the things of God as a means of escapism. We can use meetings, or singing, or music, or even Bible study. We can use all these things as a means of escapism because, it is a very interesting thing, some people will only dwell on the *things* that they feel are rosy and pleasant and nice. It's a form of escapism. They will *not* face up to harsh realities, but the harsh realities will, in the end, catch up with them. So, you and I, we need to take *heed* to this word: "Brethren, you are not in darkness, that that day should overtake you as a thief: we are all sons of light, and sons of the day: we are not of the night, nor of darkness; so then let us not sleep, as do the rest, but let us watch and be sober. For they that sleep, sleep in the night: and they that are drunken are drunken in the night. But let us, since we are of the day, put on the breastplate of faith and love."

The Breastplate of Faith and Love

Is it not interesting that there are two matters that we are told in the Word of God will characterise the end time? One is: "the love of the many will wax cold," Matthew 24:12. The other is the Lord Jesus said, "When the Son of Man comes to the earth, shall he find faith?" Luke 18:8. Now, He didn't mean He shall not find saving faith because if you look at the story He told, it is overcoming faith, enduring faith, importunate faith. Because of this, believers have flung the glove in and said, "Oh dear, dear, dear, dear, dear! In the time of the end there's going to be no love, everybody's love is going to grow cold, and there's going to be no faith!" The Lord Jesus never said that. He said the love of the many will wax cold, not the love of everyone. So why just relegate yourself to the majority? Why not be amongst that remnant that at least know something of a love growing more and more until the day of his appearing? When the Lord spoke about finding faith, He asked the question, "Shall the Son of Man find faith when He comes to the earth?" Well, we should answer, "By Your grace, Lord, You'll find it in me!"

Here is the answer: speaking about the last days, the end time, the Apostle says, "Don't let us sleep as do the rest, for they that sleep, sleep in the night and those that are drunken are drunken in the night; but let us since we are of the day put on the breastplate of *faith* and *love*." We can put on the breastplate, the thing that keeps our heart, the breastplate of faith and love, and for a helmet that thing that *guards* our mind, the hope of salvation.

The Times of the Gentiles are Over

Now I say, this is all important, this matter of the prophetic word because here the apostle Paul says in this first verse of chapter 5, "But concerning the times and the seasons, brethren, ye have no need that aught be written unto you." In other words, he felt that these Thessalonian believers were entirely clear as to the times and seasons. In fact, as a result of this letter they got into a bit of a problem, and he had to write another letter to get them out of the problem. Nevertheless, the fact is he says here, "But concerning the times and seasons ..." ("times," that is the larger periods, and "seasons," that is the smaller phases within those times) "... you do not need anything to be written to you." Do you? Are you clear about the times and epochs?

I spoke last night about the times of the Gentiles. They began with the Babylonian Empire. As far as I can see, because it is a term which speaks of the subjugation of the Jewish people, it means their subservience to Gentile domination with the emergence of a sovereign Jewish state, those times should have ended. On the 14th of May 1948, a sovereign Jewish state (whatever people may feel about it) emerged amongst the nations of the world. As far as I can see this means the times of the Gentiles are over.

Some believe that the reference of our Lord Jesus to Jerusalem being trodden down of the Gentiles until the times of the Gentiles be over means just simply trodden down by unbelievers and therefore those times will go on until His appearance. But my point is this: that when He spoke to them, He clearly spoke to the loss of their land, the loss of their statehood, and their dispersion into all the nations of the earth. Then He said that there would come a time when the domination of Jerusalem by non-Jews would be over.

"Until the times of the Gentiles be fulfilled," (Luke 21:24b). This means therefore, that not only with the emergence of the Jewish state in 1948, but the reuniting of Jerusalem and the proclamation of it as the capital of Israel, denotes that the times of the Gentiles are finished. This means, if I am right, that we have passed out of one of the great major times of world history into a last period, however long it lasts, a last phase of world history as we know it, which will culminate with the coming of the Lord Jesus. What a privilege to be alive!! There are people who have longed down through the centuries to be alive in this *era*, to actually see with their physical eyes the fulfilments of God's prophetic word. You and I have been so privileged. It is true, there are dark things, there are evil things, there are things that are horrifying. However, it is a tremendous privilege to be alive in these days and to know God's delivering power, God's enabling power, and God's anointing grace for us to overcome in these days.

Features of the End Times

Now, may I just say this on this matter: if the times of the Gentiles are over, we have passed into a last phase which we can describe as the last days, or the end times, or the threshold of the Messiah's appearing. It will be characterised by certain features. I am only going to take up one this now and another this in the next chapter and then following we will conclude. So I can't cover very much here, but these are the features you might like to consider in your own heart.

Israel: Centre of the World Stage

Israel, the state of Israel, will be at the centre of the world stage right through this last phase of human history to the coming of the Messiah. She will not only be at the heart, at the centre of the world stage, she will be the focal point of colossal conflict and antagonism on the part of the other nations. We are already witnessing that. This has been predicted by the Bible for some 2,600 years, and we are witnessing it in our generation.

Unparalleled Shaking

A second feature will be a period of unparalleled shaking on every single level of life—whether physical, or whether political, or whether military, or whether economic, or whether religious, or even spiritual. On every single level of life there will be a shaking unparalleled in the history of mankind.

New World Order

A third feature is this: there will be an emergence of a world order increasingly anti-christ in its social, moral, educational, political, and religious concepts and attitudes. We shall witness a *revolution* in morality, a *revolution* in education, a *revolution* in social behaviour and conduct, a *revolution* in religious concepts. This is a new world order which is going to emerge, and which we have already begun to see.

One World Religion

A fourth feature of this last phase will be the arrival of a false and prostituted church which will not belong to any one particular denomination, nor in my estimation will it actually be Christian. It will have Christianity as its base, but it will be a conglomeration of all the faiths of the world—Islam, Hinduism, Buddhism, Spiritism, Shintoism, Confucianism—everything the world has known wrapped into one with Christianity at its base. This will be a worldwide religion which will satisfy the needs of a new age, so it will be said.

The Man of Sin

The fifth feature of this time will be the appearance of a great saviour heading up this new order. He will seek to destroy any true knowledge of God. This is the man who is described in the Bible as the Antichrist, or the man of sin, or more blessedly described: the man destined to destruction.

Preparation of the Redeemed

Lastly, there will be a preparation of the redeemed for the coming of the Messiah. I believe that we shall see in the last phase, multitudes of people coming to know the Lord Jesus Christ. In all the wars, and upheaval, and strife, and economic recession and inflationary spiral, and more men and women, with their confidence shaken in things, will seek to find an answer to their lives and many will find the Lord—"multitudes, multitudes in the Valley of Decision," (Joel 3:14). There's no doubt in my mind about that. Also, it says the gospel will be preached in the whole world for a testimony (Matthew 24:14). It is almost in the whole world.

By modern means now, we can reach almost the whole world. Thank God for that! For that gospel is to be preached right through to the end by those who are faithful in every part of the world, in every nation, for a testimony. Then the end will come.

Upon this Rock I will Build My Church

Then, on top of that, there will be a preparation of the Bride for the coming of the Messiah. Praise God for that! Do you think that the Lord Jesus who said, "Upon this rock I will build my church and the gates of hell shall not prevail against it," (Matthew 16:18) will throw in the glove at the last point of time and say, "The enemy has proved too strong; he has defeated My work in building the church"? Never! Never! Never! The Lord Jesus' word stands forever, "Upon this rock of Myself, I will build *MY* church!" Not their church, not churches, not a denominational thing, not an institutional thing, but *HIS* Church. Upon *that* rock *He* will build His church and the gates of hell shall not prevail against it.

It is incumbent upon every true believer, *every* child of God, *every* member of the body of our Lord Jesus to rise up in faith and be with *Him* in this matter. Why should we say, "Oh dear, dear, dear the night comes when no man can work, oh! there's going to come a time when the love of the many is going to grow cold. There will be no faith in these days, we might as well finish now," and many are! They just withdraw, withdraw, and withdraw. They withdraw into a holy huddle waiting to be caught up to be with the Lord.

Oh, dear friends, that's not the church, not the church I know. She is a militant church; she is a church *terrible*! An army with banners! She is an overcoming church! Do you think that the Lord began with a bang and ends with a squeak? That at Pentecost He did something absolutely marvellous, and at the end of the age the whole thing's going to fizzle out into some little peep that one can hardly hear? *Never!* Never! I'm not talking about some universal, worldwide gathering together into some Christian system of every believer. God forbid! What I'm talking about is the preparation for the coming of the Messiah by the Spirit of God, of believers all over the world whatever name or denominational label they might have. Faithful men and women filled and anointed with the Holy Spirit, who are able to do exploits for the Lord because they have understanding of the times in which they live, and who in the last breath will overcome because of the grace of God which is given to them, and which they have appropriated to the full.

Don't let us be pessimists. Don't let us be fearful. Don't let us be negative people withdrawing, withdrawing, withdrawing as we see all the increasing immorality and paganism of western society and the strength of these great monolithic systems in other parts of the world. Why should we fear? The Most High rules in the affairs of men and Mr. Brezhnev is in the Kremlin only by the ordination of God. When the finger of God is finished with him, he will fall flat and return to dust.

Look at Mao, how powerful Mao was. They spouted morning, noon, and night Chairman Mao's thoughts, and what is he now? Dust. He's dust! He's just the same kind of dust as one of those Chinese beggars who died at the same time. That's all. In his day he had supreme power! Just like Stalin, they put his body in the Red Square in the Kremlin and they pumped all those things into him to keep him sort of there like some ... deep-frozen chicken. What is he? What is he? He's only dust. He came from the dust;

he's gone back to the dust. He awaits his final judgement before the Great White Throne of God. But every real believer has more than Stalin or Mao ever had. They have living within their mortal bodies the risen, glorified Son of God. Mao never had that, Stalin never had that, Brezhnev does not have that, nor do the other world rulers have that. You, by the grace of God, have God dwelling in you. You have been made *one* with the Eternal God in our Lord Jesus by the Spirit of God. What a privilege! Why should we fear? God is working out His purpose. If there has to come a night before the day of the Lord appears, so be it. The night will be terrible, *but* it has an end, and the daystar can arise in our hearts, touching us with glory, touching us with that blessed hope of His appearing, touching us with renewed vitality and faith that we might be enabled to do the works of God in our generation until He comes.

The State of Israel

Now my dear ones, when you really look at the Word of God, you see that we have all these things that are going to be features of this last day. I'd like to just dwell on one. Some of you may sink as I do so, but I shall dwell on one of these for a little while, and that feature is the state of Israel.

The Fig Tree: The Herald of Summer

The Lord Jesus said, "From the fig tree learn its lesson" or, "learn the parable of the fig tree." Mark 13:28, 29. What did He mean? Did He simply mean as He went on to say, "When you see these things come to pass know ye that He is nigh, even at the door"?

So is the lesson of the fig tree that as you see the fig tree putting out its leaves, its branches becoming tender and green, filled with sap, you will know that when these things begin to come to pass that His coming is right at the door?

It is an interesting thing for those of you who are Bible students (and I hope all of you are, or at least those of you who are young in the Lord are beginning to become such) to note that the fig tree in Israel is not the harbinger or herald of spring; it is the harbinger and herald of summer. The tree that is the first tree to put out its leaves in Israel is the almond tree. When the almond tree puts out its leaves at the beginning, normally, of February, we know that summer is about two months away. But when the fig tree puts out its leaves, we know that within a week or two, summer is suddenly going to descend upon us. Do you understand that? When the Lord Jesus spoke of the fig tree, He didn't mean you have three months (I'm not giving actual time, you understand what I mean). He wasn't saying you have a whole longer period of time in which to get ready and do everything and get prepared, but He was actually saying when the fig tree puts forth its leaves the Lord is very near. He is at the door! He is on the threshold! He's not coming up the street, He's not just arriving, as it were, at the other side of town, He's on the threshold! He's at the door about to come in. We have very little time, therefore.

But just let me ask again. What is this parable of the fig tree? It is most interesting. Obviously the Lord Jesus was summing up the whole of this discourse, which by the way is the major discourse the Lord ever gave on the events of the end and of His coming. It is interesting that He says in all three synoptic gospels, "Learn the lesson of the fig tree." When Luke records it in chapter

21:29—31— he is not afraid to put in a commentary now and again for our understanding—he put it like this, "When you see the fig tree and all the trees putting forth their leaves, know ye that He is nigh, even at the door." Some people have said, "You see, Luke was trying to destroy the idea that this fig tree had anything to do with the Jewish people." But I would say that the way Luke puts it makes it even more emphatic. If he had said, "When you see all the trees putting forth their leaves," then I would have said, "Ah, Luke is helping our understanding of this statement of the Lord Jesus." However, he did not say that. He said: There are two things in this fig tree. There is first of all the fig tree itself, and secondly the bursting out of leaves, which is common to all trees." Do you understand? So, we have a two-fold significance in this lesson, even more interesting if you are following me.

In Mark's gospel, chapters 11, 12, and 13, those three chapters cover a period of only two days. Two days—have you got that clear? Three chapters covering two actual days of time. On the first of those days Jesus saw a fig tree and He acted out a parable over it. Do you remember? He went up to the fig tree and went through the charade of looking for fruit (Mark 11:13,14, 20–22). Some people tell us, "Ah, well, now you see, you can tell whether the fig tree is going to bear fruit because it has little brats, right where the leaf comes into the stem and if they're there, you know it's going to bear fruit. May I tell you something? Those are a Spanish form of fig tree which was not known in Israel in the time of Jesus. We have both of these two fig trees in Israel. The other fig tree, which we also have is a fig tree which is common and indigenous to the land of Israel and does not have those little nodules next to the stem. So, it's no good trying to excuse the Lord Jesus on this.

People say, "Oh, what a dreadful thing to do. He went over there and looked through it all and couldn't find anything to eat and then He cursed it in a fit of anger." Those who are liberals and modernists tell us, "Well, you know, when people are hungry, they get irritable," This is true. It's written down in black and white, printed in certain theological books: "Jesus was a man that like the rest of us," they say. "How comforting and because He was very hungry at this time," (strangely enough He had only just had breakfast, but never mind) "He went through the charade of looking through the tree and then He cursed it in a fit of irritation and anger."

Do you believe the Lord Jesus is like that? I don't. Do you think the Lord Jesus is as dim as that? I don't. Not the Lord Jesus I know. As if the Lord Jesus was taken in by the fig tree. When He went over to that fig tree it was like His school lesson of biology. *He acted out a parable on that fig tree.* He looked for the fruit. He said, "Can you find any fruit?" Nobody could find any fruit. The disciples who recorded it, put it in for our instruction: "for it was not the season for fruit." In other words, He was doing it deliberately! Then He said, "No man may eat fruit from you anymore." Then He went into the temple and do you remember what happened in the temple? He met the authorities in the temple, and He overturned all the money changers' tables, released the doves, let out the oxen and so on, and caused a tremendous turmoil in the temple. He made a whip of cords and drove them all out of the temple saying, "My Father's house shall be called a house of prayer for all nations; you have made it a den of robbers and thieves," (Mark 11:15–17).

Then they went back to stay the night in Bethany. The next morning, going over the same path, Peter said, "Master, Rabbi, look! The fig tree is withered from its roots!" Jesus said it was a matter of faith, not meaning that if you have faith, you can curse fig trees, but meaning that the reason why that tree was fruitless and had withered from its roots was unbelief! He then went into the temple and had His confrontation with the three major religious and political groups of the nation. First the Herodians, the Royal party, then the Sadducees, and then the Pharisees. Do you remember? It ended with the greatest message of denunciation Jesus ever uttered. Those words He concluded with, "O Jerusalem, Jerusalem, that killeth the prophets and stoneth them that are sent unto her! how often would I have gathered you as a hen gathers her chicks under her wings, but ye would not! Behold, your house is left unto you desolate: and I say unto you, you shall no more see Me until you shall say, 'Blessed is He that comes in the name of the Lord,'" (Matthew 23:37–39)

Then He went out of the temple gate, down into the Kidron Valley, up onto the Mount of Olives. As they went out the disciples said, "Master, isn't this an amazing building? They've been building it for 43 years and it's still not finished." And He said, "Do you see it? Not one stone shall remain on another in the day of its judgment."
Matthew 24:1–2

Down they went into the Kidron, up onto the Mount of Olives, and leaving eight of them somewhere lower down, probably in what we now know as the Garden of Gethsemane in that area,

He went right up higher where He sat down with the four of the inner circle: Andrew, Peter, James, and John. Then they said to Him, "Master, when will these things be? When will this temple be destroyed, and what will be the sign of your coming and the end of the age?" Matthew 24:3.

Then He began, masterfully, in a few words to describe certain things which can be both applied to the destruction of the temple and the dispersion of the Jewish people *and* to the end of the age at the same time. At the end of it all, He said, "Now, learn the parable of the fig tree." Do you mean to tell me that in those men's minds, those four disciples' minds, that fig tree which had been judged the day before and which they had had riveted in their attention by Peter that morning because it had withered, not from without but from within, not by a blight, but from something in its roots, that they did not have that in their mind when Jesus said to them, "Now from the fig tree learn its lesson"?

The Major Sign: The Return to the Land

If you haven't followed me thus far, get this point because at least this will help you. What the Lord Jesus was saying is this: There are two things. When you see these things I have spoken about—the gospel being preached in all the nations, worldwide persecution, the emergence of the Antichrist, the abomination of desolation standing where it ought not to stand, wars and rumours of wars, kingdom rising against kingdom, nation against nation, famines, not just famines of food, but of energy, of basic raw materials, earthquakes in many places, when you see all these things they are like the fig tree bursting into leaf.

But there is *a* sign which is *the* confirmation of these other events. Don't be taken in because there will be wars and rumours of wars all through the thousands of years that lie ahead. There will be earthquakes, there will be famines, there will be persecution, there will be many of these things. There will be tyrants who may appear to be the Antichrist. Do not be taken in by any of these things, for there is one sign which validates the rest, and that sign is to do with the Jewish people. When they return to their land, when a sovereign Jewish state re-emerges, then know that in conjunction with these other signs, the last period of human history has arrived.

One of the reasons why people despise the prophetic word, or ignore the prophetic word, is that all through the years there have been people who believe that their generation is going to see the coming of the Lord. Isn't it true? We hear it again and again. I remember speaking to theological professors and doctors not so very far from here on one occasion and they poured scorn on it. They said, "Listen, we've heard this." One of them said, "When I was a boy, we heard this. It hasn't happened." One other said, "You know the apostle Paul thought Jesus was coming back, and He didn't, in *his* day."

Why are people "at sea"[1] on this matter? Think for a while. Be honest. Be realistic. When has this world been without war and rumours of war?" The only reason we don't know about it is we never had television and radio. When there was an enormous war in the Far East the people in the Far West didn't know anything about it for months, and months, and months,

---

1 This is a phrase meaning "in an uncertain position and in danger of becoming lost."

and months. Earthquakes. Famines. These things have been part of human life all through these thousands of years. There is only one sign which has *never* been fulfilled in all those 2000 years. In the last two millennia there has never been the re-creation of a sovereign Jewish state with Jerusalem as its capital. That has been in this generation. Now do you begin to understand? It is that sign which is *the* confirmation of all the others. In other words, when we have wars, and rumours of wars, and earthquakes, and famines, and pestilences, and persecution, and at the same time a sovereign Jewish state emerges amongst the nations of the world, that fig tree which is withered from its roots has now suddenly been resurrected. It has been, as it were, renewed. Sap has come up into the dead branches, and in a miraculous way leaves have started to come out on the tree. When that happens, know that He is nigh, even at the door.

Israel: God's Divine Time Clock

I want to just say three other things that I believe will be of help to you. You see, Israel is God's divine time clock. God's divine time clock. I want to tell you, I feel desperately sorry for those Christians who consider this whole matter of Israel as the fulfilment of God's word to be fanciful nonsense. I feel desperately sorry for them. They remove from themselves the only means by which we can tell at what hour we are in. In every other generation people could have taken some of these signs and said, "You know, I think the Lord is coming." But this matter of the Jewish people and Israel is the one sign which is infallible and validates the rest. By this, by what is happening with the Jewish people, what is happening with Israel, we can tell exactly where we are in God's divine programme.

Altogether apart from that, those who believe this is nonsense or are in error, they remove from themselves a source of tremendous confidence and encouragement in the relevance and accuracy of God's Word. I have trodden in towns and cities and villages, which for 2,600, and in some cases 3000 years have been under the sand and now are rebuilt and reinhabited with gardens and trees and parks and squares, *exactly* as God said it would be. "They shall build the old waste cities, the desolations of many generations," (Isaiah 61:4).

What an encouragement to faith it is, when God said in Zephaniah chapter 2:7, "And the remnant of the house of Judah shall lie down in the houses of Ashkelon in the evening and the coast of Ashkelon and Ashdod shall be for the remnant of the House of Judah; they shall keep their flocks there and they shall farm the land." What a thrill it is to walk into the rebuilt city of Ashkelon into the main square of Afridar at its heart, and see there in Hebrew, on a stone the words of Zephaniah the prophet, for this place of Ashkelon was never inhabited by Jews when they returned from Babylon. They avoided it because it was so Gentile. In the times of the Lord Jesus, He never visited Ashkelon because Herod the Great was born there and it was considered to be too pagan and too Gentile. Just as He never went into Tiberius, the city, for the same reason He never went into Ashkelon. Now for the first time in history, in 1957, Ashkelon has been rebuilt as an entirely Jewish city of some 75–80 thousand inhabitants. There in its central square on rock engraved in Hebrew are the words of Zephaniah the prophet: "The remnant of the House of

Judah shall lie down in the houses of Ashkelon at evening." It has been literally fulfilled!

It speaks of Ashdod and Gath and Ekron, these Philistine cities becoming Jewish homes, Jewish towns, Jewish cities. Ashdod is now the main major port of Israel a totally Jewish city of 100,000 people. Gath, of Goliath's fame, the great Philistine city is now the centre of Israeli weaving, the textile industry, a totally Jewish city. Ekron is still a small village, but at least it has been rebuilt. The only place that hasn't got a big Jewish population is Gaza. These words have been fulfilled!

It is a milestone we have passed. Hear me again, it is a divine milestone that we have passed in the re-creation of the Jewish state on the 14th of May, 1948 against all odds. We have passed a milestone in the divine programme, and by this milestone we can tell where we are. We have now passed irreversibly into the last days of the age. Praise God! It means it won't be long before we see our Messiah face to face.

From the Ends of the Earth

There's much more I could say on this matter when I take these many Scriptures. I think of those that you know so well in Isaiah 43:5,6 where it says: "Fear not, I will gather thee from the East and from the West, I will say to the North give up and to the South keep not back, bring my sons from far and my daughters from the end of the earth." You know they have come from at least 87 different countries of the world as far apart as New Zealand is from Alaska, and Chile is from Siberia. Even from China they have come back. We have a whole kibbutz of Chinese Jews. They have come back from every part of the earth.

For those who say, "Oh, but you must spiritualise these things." Yes, I believe in getting every bit of spiritual value we can. God is gathering His people into one, isn't He? From the ends of the earth, He's bringing us into the oneness of the Lord Jesus, but there is a literal fulfilment too. Let me give you a scripture in Isaiah 49:12 if you're argumentative. It says there, "Lo, these they shall come from far; from the north and from the west; and these from the land of Sinim." How do you spiritualise the land of Sinim? I've never heard a message on "these from the land of Sinim." Yet it's there in the Word of God. Then why is it in the Word of God? Has God sort of gone to sleep for a moment and a little phrase got into the Word which ought not to be there that has no relevance for anybody in anytime: "these from the land of Sinim?" Modernists tell us that it must be something to do with northern Egypt or Phoenicia (that is, Lebanon). Nonsense! Gesenius, the great Jewish Hebrew scholar says "Sinim is China." In modern Hebrew we speak of "Sin," that is China, "Sinim," that is the Chinese, "Sinet," is the Chinese language. Any Israeli reading his Bible in Hebrew sees, "And these from the land of the Chinese." Do you know how many returned from the land of the Chinese to Israel at its creation? Thirty thousand became Israeli citizens in 1948. Most of them were not Chinese of course, but from western Europe and had lived for many centuries in the ports of China. However, they came back, and the word was literally fulfilled.

A Little State, a Strong Nation

In Jeremiah 31 it says, "And their rulers shall be from amongst themselves and amongst them shall rise up rulers." In 2000 years we had not had Jewish presidents, Jewish kings, Jewish rulers, a Jewish government, or a Jewish army. We have never had such things. We've always been under foreign kings, foreign dukes, and non-Jewish emperors. Always their armies have been non-Jewish. That's where we have always been, but in this last 35 years we have a Jewish president, a Jewish prime minister, a Jewish cabinet, a Jewish government, a Jewish house of parliament, a Jewish navy, air force, and army.

You know in Micah 4:6,7 it says, "And I will make the laymen afflicted a strong nation." Israel is only 4,000,000 people, and yet may I say to you that she has become an amazing little nation that has caught the attention of the whole world. If you open your newspaper, you will find Israel somewhere on the front page. Turn on the television, Israel will be somewhere in the news, even in American news! Turn on the radio, somewhere you'll find Israel. Isn't it always so that a Jewish prime minister is coming to see a president of the United States? Quite often, I think. A little nation!

Oh, take that famous debating hall, the United Nations Organisation. It seems to spend most of its time debating this little nation of 4,000,000 people, with the territory the size of the state of Indiana. What has happened? Forty years ago, there was no Israel! Think! Forty years ago, there was no Israel! Eighty years ago people would have laughed themselves silly if you'd said, "There's going to be a Jewish state, with a Jewish president, and a Jewish prime minister, and the whole world will be talking about it." People would have laughed at you. Now the miracle has happened in this generation, and this little state has become a strong nation. It is an amazing thing to me, not something I would personally glory in, but it is an amazing thing to me that the Israeli defence forces are third in strength behind the United

States and the Soviet Union, greater than the military strength of Britain or France. We have more tanks than France, Germany, Holland, and Belgium put together, and we have more planes. Of course you Americans will say, "Well, we supply them." Anyway, whether that is so or not, the fact remains that God's Word says, "I will make the afflicted and the lame a strong nation." It has come to pass.

50 years, Jubilee

Well, dear friends, I could go on talking and talking. I could talk to you about coincidences, seeming coincidences. You know, in 1897 Theodore Herzl at the First Congress of the Zionist movement said this: "Today, we are here to lay the foundation stone of the structure that will house the Jewish nation." In his diary that night he wrote, "Today, I have founded the Jewish state. If I were to say this out loud it would be greeted with howls of laughter by the whole world, but in five years perhaps, certainly within 50, the whole world will know it." It was exactly 50 years later in November of 1947, that by a two-thirds majority vote in the United Nations, Israel was recognised as a sovereign state amongst the states of the world. Jubilee, 50 years, Jubilee. That which began with an anthem, and began with a flag, and began with an ideal, and no territory, and no state, and no army, and no government, in 50 years God brought it to pass.

In 1967, the Israeli defence forces, in a lightning move, took the old city of Jerusalem and reunited it with the rest of Jerusalem. What was happening? It is an amazing thing. In 1917, on December 11th, 1917, General Allenby of the allied forces went into Jerusalem bare headed to receive the surrender of the Turkish armies. For the first time in 700 years Islam had given up Jerusalem. Do you know the thrill that went through the great Jewish population of Jerusalem? It is a fallacy that there is only a majority of Jews in Jerusalem in the last few years; two-thirds of the population was Jewish in 1917. Do you know the thrill that went through them? Why? Because it *happened* to be, the first day of Hanukkah. Or is that a *coincidence?* Hanukkah is the festival of freedom in which we celebrate the great divine deliverance through the Maccabees over the original antichrist, Antiochus IV Epiphanes in 165 BC. Can you believe that it happened on that day, after 700 years of Islamic domination and do you know 50 years later, listen, 50 years later in June 1967, in a lightning move, Jerusalem became Jewish!? The year of Jubilee is the year in which all territory and property returns to its rightful owner. Is it a coincidence, or is God speaking? Is it another milestone we have passed so that we know the times of the Gentiles really are over?

On the sixth of October 1973, a war was launched suddenly upon Israel on two fronts that should have meant the destruction of the Jewish state, but in a miraculous intervention of God, Israel was delivered. It was the Yom Kippur War. At that time I was there and part of it. What I witnessed and what I felt in my bones as I saw it all happening before my eyes, was that we have passed another milestone! The world will never again be the same! I went everywhere telling people, "The world will never be the same!" Many Christian leaders laughed at me. They said, "Don't talk nonsense." I don't think people laugh today. The growth of international terrorism, the enormous inflationary spiral, the recessions that the whole free world is staggering from one after another, the deteriorating international situation, the nearness of a global conflict, all these things have started with 1973. We have passed into an era of oil being used as a blackmail weapon, and the gold that the Arab nations have being used to be able to pressurise the whole world and hold it hostage. We are in the run up to far more serious wars and conflicts in my estimation.

Now there are those who believe we shall not see them; we should be raptured before that comes. I suspect that we will see them, at least one further World War before, but I may be wrong. It doesn't worry me so long as we are all ready. For if we are taken up to be with the Lord, thank God, you can come to me and say, "Brother Lance, you were wrong," and I shall smile from ear to ear. But if by chance we have to go through another global conflict and we are ready, thank God for that! We are not sleeping as the rest sleep in the night, nor are we drunk as the rest are drunken in the night, but we are of the day. We have woken up.

Three milestones and we have passed them, so we know, at least in principle, where we are. We have passed into the last phase of world history. Dear people of God, let's rise up. Let's not be defeatist. Let's not be negative. Let's not be fearful. Let us rise up and let the Holy Spirit do His work in us and upon us to make us those that He can use in these days to bring others to know the Lord Jesus Christ, to build up the body of our Lord Jesus, to equip us for what lies ahead. May the Lord help us. We have been given the word of prophecy as a lamp shining in a dark place, whereunto ye do well that you take heed until the day dawn and the daystar arise in your hearts (II Peter 1:19).

Shall we pray?

Heavenly Father, You know just where we are. You know every one of our hearts. You know, Lord, our state of readiness or unreadiness; have mercy upon us Lord. We are so weak and so dim at times and so easily misled, and sometimes Lord we are those who misinterpret things. Have mercy, Lord, upon us and in Your wonderful grace, reach every single person. May we be challenged, Lord, simply to put things right. May we be those, Lord, in whose lives all the issues have been settled, who have surrendered to Yourself in totality, who are being prepared and made ready for the days that lie ahead. Oh, Lord may we be energised to build one another up in our most holy faith. May we become functioning members of the body of our Lord Jesus Christ. May we become a community wherever we are found as believers that holds forth the word of life to the dying multitudes around us. Oh, Heavenly Father, use this time this morning to further Your own interests and fulfil Your own plan for us. We ask it in the name of Jesus. Amen.

4.
Receiving An Unshakable Kingdom

Hebrews 12:25–29

See that ye refuse not him that speaketh. For if they escaped not when they refused him that warned them on earth, much more shall not we escape who turn away from him that warneth from heaven: whose voice then shook the earth: but now he hath promised, saying, Yet once more will I make to tremble not the earth only, but also the heaven. And this word, Yet once more, signifieth the removing of those things that are shaken, as of things that have been made, that those things which are not shaken may remain. Wherefore, receiving a kingdom that cannot be shaken, let us have grace, whereby we may offer service well-pleasing to God with reverence and awe: for our God is a consuming fire.

Shall we just bow together in a word of prayer? Let us really unite to ask the Lord to be with us as we turn to His word and to meet us in it.

Heavenly Father, we just want to thank You that when we turn to Your word, You have made provision for us so that, Lord, this may not be futile or misspent in any single part. We pray that Your plan for this evening time may be fulfilled Lord, and that Your word may come to us in a living and vital and powerful manner so that, Lord, both in the speaking and in the hearing, it may be Your ability and power which is apparent. Dear Lord, You know that if I speak in my own energy and if we hear in our own ability then, Lord, it will not amount to much, but we praise You, Lord, that You have said that him that has an ear to hear what the Spirit says to the churches, hear. Dear Lord, we pray together that those ears of our spirit may be open to hear Your voice. We want to be a people who have an understanding of the days in which we live and know what You are requiring of us. So, dear Heavenly Father, we do commit our time to You, we pray that You would fill this whole time Lord, shutting us in with Yourself so that we may hear Your voice and know Your speaking and working. We ask all this in the name of our Lord Jesus. Amen.

I would like to speak about another feature that will characterise these last days of the age, which is an unparalleled shaking of every single aspect of life. Now, this is very, very important for believers because whether the Lord comes sooner or later during this phase, the fact remains that once everything begins to be shaken to pieces, believers are not going to be exempt from that shaking. They are all going to be in it and part of it. Therefore, it is very, very necessary to know that one of the features, one of the characteristics of the days into which we are moving, is this determination of God to shake everything that can be shaken to pieces. Now will you please note that? It is not the devil who is shaking everything to pieces, nor is it Marxism that is shaking everything to pieces, nor is it Capitalism that is shaking everything to pieces, nor is it flesh and blood that is shaking everything to pieces, nor new ideologies. It is God who has said, "I will shake, not only the earth, but the heavens also." It will be of great comfort to us if we recognise the simple fact that the one who is behind the shaking is our Lord and God. Then we shall understand that there is a purpose in it, and we are receiving a kingdom that cannot be shaken.

For us who know the Lord, the great requirement is that we should get to know the unshakable and invincible King, the Lord Jesus, for the more we get to know Him, the more unshakable our lives will be. He will see to it by the Spirit of God that we are founded upon that Rock and when the storm comes, we will not be moved or carried away.

Now, this is a very important matter that we are now considering, and I am trusting the Lord to give the grace that is required to be able to really communicate to you something of what the Word of God says about this shaking.

A Physical Shaking

This shaking is in the first place a physical shaking. Now, I want to make this quite clear. In the last and final stage of this shaking, it will be a physical shaking. So, although it is of great value to spiritualise this shaking and talk about the shaking of political things, economic things, spiritual things, religious things, and moral things, we must recognise the fact that the Word of

God proclaims that, in the last phase of the end time, the heavens themselves are going to be shaken. Stars are going to fall out of their orbit, something is going to happen to the sun, something is going to happen to the moon, something is going to happen to the oceans and the tides. Everything is going to go, as it were, skew-whiff, if you understand my English English. (I understand that earlier today I mystified the whole crowd by use of the word "blancmange." A blancmange is something that is made for dessert, a sweet dessert made with milk. I hope that helps you all. You really ought to know your English better. It is a very ordinary word.)

This shaking of the heavens and the earth we find in all places. First in Luke 21:25–26:

> *And there shall be signs in sun and moon and stars; and upon the earth distress of nations, in perplexity for the roaring of the sea and the billows; men fainting for fear, and for expectation of the things which are coming on the world: for the powers of the heavens shall be shaken.*

Now, it may be of value sometimes to spiritualise this sea roaring and everything else, but in the first place it is literal. There is going to be something happening in sun and moon and stars which will in turn affect the oceans and the tides. The powers of the heavens are going to be shaken. Look again at Matthew 24:29, 30:

> *But immediately after the tribulation of those days the sun shall be darkened, and the moon shall not give her light, and the stars shall fall from heaven, and the powers of the*

heavens shall be shaken: and then shall appear the sign of
the Son of man in heaven: and then shall all the tribes of
the earth mourn, and they shall see the Son of man coming
on the clouds of heaven with power and great glory.

Again, in Peter's great message on the day of Pentecost, quoting the prophet Joel. In Acts 2:19–21:

And I will show wonders in the heaven above,
And signs on the earth beneath;
Blood, and fire, and vapor of smoke:
The sun shall be turned into darkness,
And the moon into blood,
Before the day of the Lord come,
That great and notable day:
And it shall be, that whosoever shall call on
the name of the Lord shall be saved.

Behind the Shaking

Now, we know that this prophecy began to be fulfilled on the day of Pentecost. However, we also know that this prophecy of Joel was not exhaustively fulfilled on the day of Pentecost because although something did happen to the sun, nothing happened to the moon, and there were not pillars or billows of cloud on the earth. We are told that in the last phase of this age that something will happen to the sun, something will happen to the moon, there will be billows of cloud of smoke or whatever, on the earth, and it says that the sun shall be turned into darkness and the moon into blood. So, now we have at least three examples apart from the Hebrews 12 prediction of a physical shaking of the universe, so tremendous that everything, as it were, will just go out of its routine order. Now, it is interesting, Matthew and Mark speak of this shaking *following* a period of great distress and tribulation and *preceding* the Messiah's coming. Luke speaks of this great shaking following the end of "the times of the Gentiles" and ushering in the Messiah's coming. Joel speaks of this shaking immediately preceding that great and glorious day of the Lord.

Now all these signs are interrelated. If something happens to the sun, to the light of the sun, it will immediately have an effect on the moon. If something happens to the moon, it will immediately have an effect on the oceans and the tides in particular. Have you understood that? So, all these things are actually interrelated. Something only needs to be done to the sun and it, in turn, will affect the moon which, in turn, will affect the tides, the oceans, and the seasons. So, I hope this is clear that the final stage of this predicted shaking is a physical shaking of the earth. I cannot imagine anything more designed to shake the confidence of humanistic man than something happening in the heavens. In spite of the Space Age, in spite of all his technological skill, if something were to go wrong with the sun, a fear would seize the greatest and most intelligent minds in this world because it is beyond their scope to cope with, and it is God who is behind this shaking. It is God who is behind this shaking.

I find this very interesting because it means this: man is, I believe, perfectly at rest, in one sense, if one could so speak, when he knows that these disturbances are the result of his own actions. In other words, disturbances are the result of war, the result of some kind of dislocation of life; even though it may bring death and horror, he is still aware that he has done it. However, when it is something that is nothing to do with man, something that went wrong with the heavens themselves, then he fears because it is beyond his scope. It is beyond the range of his understanding. Suddenly, he realises that he is a finite, created being in a universe that is beyond his power to control. So, God has foreordained that in the final phase of this age, He will shake the physical universe so that man may know that there is a God, and that he (man) is not the be-all and end-all of everything.

Destabilising Human Society

Having said that, I would like to say a little more about this shaking because I have said it is the final stage. There is, in fact, a shaking which is foreordained by God. A shaking of every form and every aspect of life: political, economic, educational, religious, social, moral, or spiritual. God intends to shake to pieces everything in this present world order. He is the One who has said He will do it.

In Matthew chapter 24, and of course, in all the three synoptic gospels, but in Matthew 24:6–8 we read these words of Jesus, "And ye shall hear of wars and rumours of wars; see that ye be not troubled: for these things must needs come to pass; but the end is not yet. For nation shall rise against nation, and kingdom against kingdom; and there shall be famines and earthquakes in divers places. But all these things are the beginning of travail."

That which our Lord Jesus predicts is interesting: war, rumours of war, revolution, civil war, earthquakes, famines, and plagues. Now, all of this has been the common lot of human history.

It is not as if any century of the last 2000 years has been free from this kind of thing. There have always been these kinds of things, but evidently, at the end of the age, the Lord will see to it that there is a combination of these things, quite unique in its intensity and fierceness, so that the whole of human life is shaken. These are the things that destabilise society. War, rumours of war, revolution, civil war—all these things destabilise human society. They create upheavals. They bring about a breakdown of social and moral standards. In history, anyone will tell you that these are the things which break up the routine of normal living. It is interesting that our Lord Jesus speaks not only of these things, but of earthquakes. They are a destabilising factor. When an earthquake is big enough, it can be a very destabilising factor. Famine. I think those of you with Chinese background will remember from your history that there have been famines in China that have been colossal in their influence. They are in themselves a destabilising factor. Now, we are talking about not only famine of food, but we are talking about shortages. It may be shortages of raw materials. It may be shortages of energy. There are all kinds of things that we could call famines, but they all end in the same thing: a destabilising of society, the breaking up of the normal routine of life, whether it is national, international, or local.

The Beginning of Travail

Our Lord Jesus speaks of these things, not as the end. He says, "... but the end is not yet." In fact, He goes farther and says, "... these things are the beginning of the end," and He uses—oh, the grace of the Lord Jesus, for those who are sensitive to the words He uses—He uses the most marvellous words to describe these horrifying things. He says, "... these are the beginning of travail."

If I were to put it another way, it may bring it home to you, "these are the beginning of the birth pangs." Birth pangs of what? "Oh," says someone, "birth pangs of horror?" No, birth pangs of the Kingdom! It is the beginning of the birth pangs of the Kingdom. I think that is marvellous. Any of you who are mothers know something about the birth pangs. You know that there may be a number of such birth pangs, but in the end, it ends in a birth, and it ends in joy. It ends in new life. The Lord Jesus describes all this shaking, and all these things which will destabilise human society and shake to pieces everything that can be shaken. He does not describe it in fearful terms, but for those of us who belong to the Lord Jesus, for our encouragement, for our strengthening, He says, "... these are the beginning of the birth pangs." They are birth pains to be endured, but the end will be glory. The end will be the coming of the Messiah. The end will be the coming of the Kingdom of God and in the end, that new heaven and new earth in which righteousness dwells.

I think it is just wonderful to consider this whole matter like this. If you are all going to get fearful and say, "Oh dear, what a morbid ending to this conference. First we talked about one thing and then about another, and now we have got the great shaking. Everything is going to be shaken. What a prospect!" Some of you youngsters who are going to get married in this year or set up a new home, or those of you who have just been married in the last year and say, "What a prospect for us! Everything is going to be shaken to pieces."

It is a question of where your treasure is. If your treasure is down here, you are going to be fearful because you are in for a bad time. If you want to gather together as much gold as you can down here, you are in for a rough time. (I am not against gathering gold myself, down here. I do not see anything particularly wrong with it, if you are a good steward of it.) However, if that is the be-all and end-all of your life, then you are in for a very sad and unhappy future in these next years. If your treasure is in the Lord Jesus, and if you are seeking His Kingdom and His righteousness, then your home can be a centre for the comfort and the strengthening of not only other believers, but a place where unsaved men and women in desperation can find the salvation of God. Because you have an inward stability in a destabilised society, a rock-like quality which only God can give you, you can hold forth the Word of life to others, and others can come to know God through you.

Call Upon the Name of the Lord

Is it not interesting that in the prophecy of Joel quoted by Peter on that day of Pentecost it says, "... and whosoever shall call upon the name of the Lord shall be saved"? It is speaking not only for the whole age, but for those days when something happens in sun, and moon, and on the earth. Anyone who calls upon the name of the Lord shall be saved. Oh, for those who will provoke others to call upon the name of the Lord. Others in whom those who are without God and without Christ see a peace that passes understanding, and a joy unspeakable and full of glory, and a more abundant life, and an exceeding greatness of divine power that will provoke them to discover the same Lord and Saviour. Let us not look upon the negative and dark side in this whole thing. Personally, I hope the Lord gets on with it as quickly as is possible. Shake the whole thing to pieces! We are all living in a fool's paradise, especially in the States and Canada where everything is so good. We are living in a fool's paradise, and we tend to put our trust in the stability of society. Yet underneath it is only a façade; underneath is all the avarice and wickedness of fallen man. It has to be shaken to pieces so that that which cannot be shaken might be made manifest.

The shakings that we are talking about are the birth pangs of His coming Kingdom, and I say that is something to look forward to, that is something to lift up our heads and to praise God about. Don't you think?

Constituents of the Shaking

May I say something about this shaking and the constituents of it? I hope it will not be boring, I hope it will help you to understand the whole contemporary nature of this thing.

World War I

In my estimation, the shaking began in this century with the First World War of 1914 to 1918. That World War—which was to suck into its orbit, like a whirlpool, all the empires of Europe, except the British, and destroy them—was a war that no one expected, and no one wanted, so historians tell us. It was as if an unseen mastermind trapped them, so that, in the end, they were locked in a war that they did not want, and the flower of the manhood of Europe and Britain died on the battlefields.

Until that war, world society had more or less continued as it had done for century upon century. Indeed, we could almost say that there was nearly 1000 years of a kind of progress, but it was the same kind of society, basically. However, at the end of the 1914–18 war, a whole way of life had been swept away which has never again reappeared. At the end of that war, the Austro-Hungarian Empire, which stretched from the Black Sea to the Mediterranean to the Baltic, had disappeared, never to reappear. The German Reich disappeared, not to reappear. France was crippled as a result of it. The Russian Empire with its Czars had disappeared, never to reappear. Just before that war began, the Chinese Empire, the oldest of all the empires, and with the longest continuous history, came to an end in 1911. It was a time of unparalleled upheaval and turmoil for world society.

Many people tend to think that the Second World War of 1939–1945 was the war which changed the face of the world, but it was not. The Second World War only finished off what was begun in the First World War. For after the First World War, most of British and European manhood that had gone into that war with some kind of belief in God, came out agnostic or atheist. There was a sudden turning away from church attendance all over Europe and in Britain and Scandinavia. The churches were more or less left empty. For the first time, the concept of man as made in the image of God (therefore accountable and responsible to God) was put on one side, and the Darwinian-Marxist theory that man is just the evolution of matter was adopted.

Marxism

By the way, let me say one other thing about that First World War. In the midst of all the turmoil and all the bloodshed and death of that First World War, there came to birth something that was destined to be one of the greatest constituents in the shaking of this century: Marxism. If the nations of Europe and Britain had not been locked in that World War, they would have all supported the Czar. They would have destroyed Bolshevism at its birth, but they were so weakened that they could do nothing about it. Therefore, in 1917, the Russian Revolution was successful, and there came onto the world scene a demonic ideology that was destined to cause rivers of blood to be shed all over the globe.

It is interesting that at the same time there was another movement in the midst of the war, in the same year. It was a declaration on the part of the British government, which has come to be known as the Balfour Declaration, declaring that Palestine should be a homeland for the Jewish people. This declaration was to lead to the birth of the Jewish state in 1948.

World War II

Now, the Second World War finished off what the First World War began. In that Second World War, weapons were used that had never ever been known before in the history of mankind. The Second World War ended with the dropping of an A-bomb on Hiroshima, in which, in one single minute, 100,000 human beings were incinerated. That Second World War changed, finally, the face of society. Men and women emerged from the Second World War with a new view of sex, a new view of chastity, a new view of morality, a new view of religion, a new view of social standards, and a new view of moral standards. All these things have come out of that Second World War.

The concept, the Darwinian and Marxist concept, as I have said, that man is merely matter, an animal evolving, has led to the legalisation of abortion, the legalisation of homosexuality, and in the end it will lead to the legalisation of euthanasia, mercy killing. If man is only an animal, an intelligent animal, but an animal, he is not made in the image of God, he is only an animal, then he can be if necessary exterminated in the same way we exterminate flies or cockroaches with as little conscience as a person might put to sleep an unwanted animal.

My dear friends, I do not believe that the world is yet ready for a world leader, and a world government, and a totally new moral order. It will require a third world war. If that war comes, then I believe you will find that the last piece of the jigsaw is in its place. Mankind will come out of that war ready for a world leader who will ban war and terrorism, and who will introduce an altogether new type of society. We can call it the lawless society, that is, a society without law. This is what is predicted by the Spirit of God in II Thessalonians 2. It speaks of the Lawless One and the Mystery of Lawlessness. It does not mean gangsterism, but amorality. Do you understand? (I think in American English you say "a-morality." I don't know, but do you understand what I am trying to say?) In other words, we are going to move into a society in which our education, our social behaviour and conduct, our medicine, our scientific progress, and every other form of human life is based on the Darwinian concept that man is only an animal. He is matter and no more. He is not made in the image of God, and he is not accountable to God.

Now let me just say a few other things about the shaking. I have spoken about two world wars and the possibility of a third. Marxism, as I have already mentioned, has been one of the greatest constituents in the shaking of the world in this 20th century. Before 1945, communism was restricted to the Soviet Union. Elsewhere, in China, for instance, and in other countries, there were small groups of dedicated communists—in some case, armies in rebellion—but small and insignificant. From 1945, those forces of Marxism took half of the free world. Wherever it came, it brought death and bloodshed and horror. No single factor in this century has caused as much shaking as has Marxism.

International Terrorism

There is something else I would like to mention, another constituent in the shaking, which is much more recent. Since the middle of the 1960s, and particularly in the 1970s, the world has witnessed a phenomenon that it has never witnessed before: international terrorism. This is the use of force on innocent people to achieve a political end, and this kind of terrorism is quite remarkable. We see dedicated young men and women of colossal ideal, believing that they are bringing in a better society, a good society, and are ready to kill, injure, and maim in order to bring in that society. They will blow up airliners with innocent people in them, they will throw bombs into restaurants, they will gun down innocent men or women, they will take hostage people who are not actually criminal or have not even done wicked things and will murder them in order to use their force as a pawn, as it were, in a game of chess. Do you understand what I am trying to say? It is amazing what this has done in the world. It is a destabilising factor.

Islamic Revival

We have yet another, and that is the Islamic revival. The Islamic revival is sweeping over one-third of the world. I do not think here in the United States you know what is happening. The Islamic Revival is one of the most amazing things to see. You see these people who are possessed—that is the only word for it. I know many people in Israel and Muslims, young men, who suddenly have been taken over by this ideology. You can see it in their eyes, there is a kind of unnatural light in their eyes, as if something is directing them and mastering them. The ladies you will notice, all of a sudden, they dress from head to foot in a certain kind of dress with a certain kind of scarf.

I first became aware of this a few years ago. I was as dumb as anybody else on it. I was in Gaza, in the southern part of Israel, and I was taking meetings. Wherever we drove, I noticed on every street corner a mosque was being built. Now, it is not hard to identify a mosque because of the minaret. When I saw all these on every street corner—sometimes in one street there would be one mosque on one end, and one mosque on the other end—I said to the dear servant of the Lord who was with me, who had lived for many years in Gaza, "What is this?" He said, "Don't you know? The whole Muslim world is in the grip of a revival, so strong that they are devoting all their money to the building of these mosques and to the training of their young people. They believe the time has come for Islam to take the world."

Now, those of you who remember the Iranian hostage-taking, the American hostages that were kept in Iran, will remember what they saw on television. These are not ordinary people. They are possessed by something, and this revival is spreading all the way from the Philippines and Malaysia in Southeast Asia all the way to Mauritania on the Atlantic Coast of West Africa. Furthermore, think of the mosques that have been built in Western Europe. Recently, £20 million sterling—something in the region of about $37 million—was spent on the building of the biggest mosque in the Western Hemisphere in Regents Park, London. It was opened in the presence of His Grace the Archbishop of Canterbury, and other ecclesiastics, who listened to Crown Prince Fahd of Saudi Arabia, now King Fahd of Saudi Arabia. In his speech, he said, "We Muslims believe that if we can take London for Islam, we can take the whole world." In Geneva, they have built a mosque with a minaret above the traditional Protestant cathedral. In Rome, a mosque has been built on the hill rising above the Vatican. Now, it does not mean anything to people in the West that minarets are higher than their church spires, but for the Muslim, the fact that a minaret is higher than a church spire, means a tremendous amount.

Two Leaders of the Islamic Revolution

You have only to take two of the leaders of this radical Islamic revolution to understand what I am talking about. The first is Ayatollah Khomeini. Do you know what Ayatollah means? Sign of God. Then, there is our Colonel Muammar Gaddafi of Libya. These two men have all the money they need from oil and all the gold they need as a result of the sales of that oil. They are the two great destabilising factors in the Muslim world. Muammar Gaddafi is behind the financing of nearly every terrorist organisation in the world. The IRA has received a large, substantial amount of its money for the purchase of its arms and explosives from

Muammar Gaddafi. The Eta Basque guerrillas have received a large and substantial sum of their money for the purchase of arms and explosives from Muammar Gaddafi. Gaddafi was the man who was paying for the terrorists to be trained in Lebanon, in the Palestinian camps. It is all part of the shaking, all part of the shaking.

Since 1973, we have seen recession, after recession, after recession. We have seen a spiralling world inflation. We have been haunted all the time on the horizon by the possibility of a monetary and gold collapse. We have a population explosion so tremendous that you cannot take it in for numbers, when you think that the population of India is doubling now every three years. You must also add, not only to the recessions, and the possibility of a monetary collapse, and the population explosion, but also, shortages of food. We have been warned, not once but again, and again, and again by the United Nations Relief Organisation that the world very shortly will begin to see such a shortage of food that thousands upon thousands of people will die. All these things are the constituents of this shaking. God has said, "I will shake not only the earth, but the heavens also." His end is to shake to pieces everything that can be shaken so that that which cannot be shaken might be made manifest.

Now, all that may seem to some of you to be rather depressing. I say again, it is where your treasure is. If your treasure is in the Lord Jesus, I will tell you something, if you do not know it, He cannot be shaken. He, if I may be so irreverent, He is the one bank in which you are absolutely safe to make deposits. There is about the Lord Jesus something immovable, unshakeable, and invincible. If you and I have a life in Him and a destiny in Him, then we shall not be shaken like the rest of the world.

Now, you do understand that all this must have some practical consequence. Turn with me to Luke 21:28, "But when these things begin to come to pass, look up, lift up your heads; for your redemption draweth nigh."

In other words, no fear, no panic is needed. You can look up, you can worship. Your redemption is drawing near. Every day in this shaking, your redemption is coming nearer. Think of it like that. It is not going to be so long. We have not got to think in terms of thousands of years. Every day brings us nearer to when our redemption is finally going to be manifest, so we can afford to worship. We can afford to stand up and bless the Lord. We can afford to straighten our backs and lift up our heads because our redemption draws near.

What are We to Do?

Then there is another thing in Hebrews 12:28, it says, "Wherefore, receiving a kingdom that cannot be shaken, let us have grace whereby we may offer service well pleasing to Him." Receiving a kingdom that cannot be shaken.

One or two of you have said to me, "Now, we have no doubt that what you have said is right and important. It is strategic. You have made us sit up, but what are we to do?" Now, just wait. What are you to do? My answer is you should do what you should have done. That is my answer. You should do what you should have done.

"Oh," you say, "well, what should I have done?" You should see that you are absolutely right with God. That is the first requirement. Our brother, Stephen, has spoken about preparation of the bride for the coming of the bridegroom, and has spoken about the need of repentance. Christians sometimes seem to find it hard to repent. There are areas in our lives where we need to be broken, where we need to yield, and where we need to surrender.

Now, when you say to me, "What should I do?" What do you expect me to say? "Oh, I know!"? I know some who would be so happy if I said to them, "Go out tomorrow and buy a store of food."

"Oh," you say, "thank you, thank you, thank you. Thank you so much, that was so practical."

You go out and you buy a store of food. Then, you would be very happy if I said to you, "See that you have a deep shelter." Or, if I said to you, "Get a book on nuclear war and read up all the things you should do." Some of you might be happy.

Should We Withdraw?

What should you do? Of course, it makes me smile sometimes because I knew some people some while ago. They were dear people, but when they heard some of these kind of things they suddenly got the idea that they should withdraw. (I have been involved with two or three groups that have withdrawn.) One rushed away from Florida, right up into the far north of Alaska, until they were shaken by an earthquake up there!

But I had an even more remarkable experience a while ago, of a group who told me that the Lord had told them to withdraw from whatever city it was, I cannot remember now. They went to live in the state of Washington ... on the slopes of Mount

St. Helens! They told me that the Lord had warned them that nuclear war was coming, and that they should withdraw and have a farm.

I suppose I have a warped sense of humour, which probably comes from my Jewish blood, but when Mount St. Helens erupted, I could not help lying on my bed and laughing when I heard that it sent up into the atmosphere more than four nuclear bombs could have done! I think sometimes when we react in the flesh to this kind of thing, we jump out of the frying pan, into the fire.

Again, it is my warped sense of humour, but I had to smile when I met a young couple, who withdrew from the rat-race in London. They went to what they thought would be a quiet life ... in the Falkland Islands! They found themselves in the midst of a war in the one spot in the whole earth where they thought they would miss any war!

My dear friends, do not do anything foolish. Do not take this kind of message and say, "We must run away. We must go somewhere in some remote part of Canada where we shall be safe." I want to tell you something from my own experience of Israeli intelligence that, in fact, some of the most strategic nerve centres of the military infrastructure of these countries are in the most remote places. You think that you have run away and are safe, and are probably in the one place where Soviet missiles are going to home in at the very first moments of any conflict.

The One Safe Way

There is only one safe way. What is it? It is to do what you should do. In other words, to do the will of God. Very simple. Do you know that all the issues in your life and my life are a matter of doing the will of God? Very often the Lord is asking you to do something, and you have just been battling on it, battling and battling for years. You say it is not important. You say, "Well, it is insignificant. It does not matter. Why does it—no, no, no it cannot be the Lord." But you know, sometimes, with some small thing that God is asking of you, it is not the thing itself that is important. It is the obedience in doing it that is so important. When God says, "Give up this, or give up that friendship, or go this way, or go that way, or do not go in this path," when you do it, to your amazement you will find that you are led, introduced into a new universe of spiritual discovery and life and power. You will not believe that such a simple step of obedience and faith could have brought you into so much. Indeed, most of us, when God has been speaking to us and we have finally done what He asked of us and we come into such blessing have said, "Why did I not do it years before?!"

What should you do? You should be right with the Lord. That is the first thing. Here is the second: while you have got time, buy as much gold, and I am not talking about physical gold, buy as much gold from Him as you can. Jesus says, "I counsel you to buy of me gold refined in the fire that you may become rich." You have time. Through experience, have your own, as it were, appropriation of the Lord Jesus. That is what you need.

Here is a third thing: whilst it is day, let us build one another up. The Scripture says, "Not forsaking the assembling of ourselves together as the manner of some is, and so much the more as you see that day approaching," (Hebrews 10:25). Fellowship is not so easy. I mean, fellowship is always a lovely thing if we can all just sort of come together and sing some lovely hymns and choruses and look at all the shining faces and the clapping hands or the upraised arms. It is a lovely thing. However, when it comes to being built together and working together and going through together, and esteeming each other better than ourselves, and humbling ourselves before one another and washing one another's feet, then it is not quite so pleasant.

What is it that God requires of you? He requires that into your life should come an unshakable kingdom. Now, dear children of God, what does that mean? What does it mean to receive a kingdom that cannot be shaken? What is a kingdom? A kingdom has a king. Let me say something else. It is a matter of authority, is it not? It is a matter of authority. How can you receive a kingdom and do your own will? How can you receive a kingdom and rebel against Him or murmur against Him? Or have an argument with Him? Or have an outstanding issue with Him? If you have an argument with the Lord Jesus, if there is some issue that you cannot settle, then your life is not unshakable and when the shaking comes, you will be shaken.

Be Right with the Lord and One Another

Dear friends, I could spend an hour just talking about the practical side of this matter. There are many more things than I am saying; I am just dealing now with the principle of the whole thing. The principle is this: you must be right with the Lord, and you must be right with one another. If we are right with the Lord and right with one another, then we are receiving a kingdom that cannot be shaken. Thank God for that and we can receive grace to offer service well pleasing to Him.

I could say other things. You young people, you must surely know that it is more and more difficult now in the academic world, in the world of education, to really be a Christian. For the concepts upon which behaviour and conduct are now based are no longer the Judeo-Christian truth but are the Darwinian-Marxist concept. Do you understand what I am saying? It means that if you are a child of God in the social sphere, or the medical sphere, or the scientific sphere, you are often made to look like some narrow-minded bigot. Old fashioned. Belonging to another age. Not forward-looking. This is where we need to help one another. We need to support one another. We need to pray for one another. We need to care for one another because you younger people are going to be in the front line of the battle. If the older ones do not understand what you are facing and cannot support you and strengthen you in prayer and fellowship, what hope is there?

A Word to Parents

You mother and fathers, let me just say one word to you. Never leave to some Sunday school or to others the spiritual education of your children. What your children learn at your knee, they will never forget. Therefore, if you are Christian mothers and fathers, give time as a priority to the teaching of your children in a living way, not in a boring, heavy, old-fashioned, Victorian manner in which you are ramming down their throats Scripture all the time. I am not talking about that. I mean a living, loving spontaneous way of educating your children in the things of God. Give time. I am unmarried, but I know more sometimes about families than some married people do. Why? Because I have a continuous stream of young people from Christian families who come to me to complain. I know more sometimes of what goes on in some of the families than the folks themselves. When children come to me, I say, "Why don't you talk with your father?"

"Father has no time for me."

"Oh," I say, "that is not true. I have heard your father pray for you."

"No, no, Father has no time for me."

"What do you mean?"

"Well, when I ask him, he is always reading the newspaper, and he says, 'Oh, don't bother me.'"

You Christian fathers, remember you have treasure in those children of yours. Never put them off. Never ignore them. Try to help them.

As for you mothers, the way I see it, the mother is the most important influence in a home. I think one of the reasons the Bible tells women to be subject to their husbands is that women are by far the most influential factor in family life. Therefore, do not be bossy. Do not try to rule your husband. Try to get the right order in your home, and above all, teach your children. Communicate with your children. Win your children so that as they grow up, they grow up your friends.

One day, not too far ahead, the whole educational system that we have known with its Christian basis will disappear. It is already nearly gone. In its place, children will be taught horrifying things. Only the influence of Christian parents will keep such children from those evils. Do you want to have to see before your eyes the fulfilments of the words that children will give up their parents to persecution?

Dear people of God, I say, I could spend a lot of time on the practical consequences of all that I am talking about because until this generation, things have more or less gone along as always. In spite of war, in spite of revolution, in spite of troubles, there has been more or less a general standard of life and a stability. You must understand that that stability has gone forever. It will never come back. Therefore, you and I have got to realistically judge a new situation. We have got to learn how to face it and how to cope with it.

The Recap

Now again, let me recap: the first thing is that you be right with the Lord and right with your brothers and sisters, whatever the price. Get right with the Lord! You will never be sorry about getting right with Him. It may cost you everything to put something right, but you will never be sorry in the days that are ahead that you did it. Get right with one another. If there is someone that you cannot have fellowship with or someone that you hate—I know that is a strong word to use for Christians but let us be realistic—someone that you detest, no matter what the price, humble yourself before that person. Get right with the Lord and get right with that person.

Then, become a contributing factor in the family of God. Do not just be a spectator. Do not be a dead weight. Do not be someone on the fringe, always a critic. Commit yourself to the Lord and to His people. Become a contributing factor. This will bring a stability into your life, and a rock-like quality into your life, as nothing else can. You will learn more through fellowship than you will ever learn in any other way. Sometimes, you will learn more of the Lord and more of His grace and His power through people you cannot get on with in the church, than ever you learn from those you love and can flow with easily. The time is far spent. Allow God to do His work in you.

In these other spheres, do not run around all over the place trying to find some safe haven. In no place will you be safer than in the will of God for you. If the will of God is in the front line, that is the safest place for you. If the will of God is at the heart of conflict, that is the safest place for you. Make sure that you are within the will of God. If you have responsibilities for children, make sure that you are communicating to them in ways that they can understand. Some of these basic truths, they will not get at school, and they will not get at university, and they will not get on a national scale. They will only get them in the home and in the assembly of God's people. So let us give ourselves to some of these things that are vitally necessary if the Lord is going to really make us a people who are receiving a kingdom that cannot be shaken. May God help you and may He help me.

Shall we pray:

Dear Heavenly Father, You know better than any of us exactly where we are heading and what is happening in the society around us. At present, Lord, we thank You that there is that which restrains the mystery of lawlessness, but, Lord, we are all very conscious that suddenly, at some point, that restraining factor is going to be taken away. Then, Lord, we shall see the appearance, not only of the lawless one, but of this whole new kind of society. Heavenly Father, prepare us as Your children for those days. We know that the coming of our Lord Jesus is drawing near, and Father, we are so thankful for it. If it should be tonight, we would rejoice, Lord, with unspeakable joy.

If it would be this week, we would be so full of joy, but, Lord, if we have to go through part of the turmoil and the shaking, and the problems that will come upon the earth, Lord, prepare us that we may be a people who are unshakeable and invincible, immovable because we know You.

Oh, Heavenly Father, You know if there are issues in different lives here in this place this evening that have not been settled. You know, Lord, if there are relationships that are not right. You know, Lord, if there are areas of bitterness or unforgiveness. Oh, Heavenly Father, by Your Holy Spirit, challenge us, that we may suddenly realise that we may have to face You, and therefore, Lord, we shall be somehow enabled to put these things right. Help us to repent where repentance is needed. Help us to act where action is required. Help us, Lord, we pray that we may be those who by Your grace overcome and do Your works in this last phase of human history. Help us, Lord, now as together we commit ourselves to You. In the name of our Lord Jesus. Amen.

5.
But Take Heed to Yourselves

Mark 13:5–8

And Jesus began to say unto them, Take heed that no man lead you astray. Many shall come in my name, saying, I am he; and shall lead many astray. And when ye shall hear of wars and rumors of wars, be not troubled: these things must needs come to pass; but the end is not yet. For nation shall rise against nation, and kingdom against kingdom; there shall be earthquakes in divers places; there shall be famines: these things are the beginning of travail.

Mark 13:9

But take ye heed to yourselves: for they shall deliver you up to councils; and in synagogues shall ye be beaten; and before governors and kings shall ye stand for my sake, for a testimony unto them.

Mark 13:22

for there shall arise false Christs and false prophets, and shall

show signs and wonders, that	**Mark 13:33**
they may lead astray, if possible,	*Take ye heed, watch and pray:*
the elect.	*for ye know not when the time is.*

Shall we bow together in a word of prayer?

Heavenly Father, we want to thank You this morning that we can turn to You as we come to Your word and we want to once again thank You, that You have made provision for us in a specific manner. We would avail ourselves of that provision, of that anointing, both for speaking and for hearing, make this last time of this particular conference a very blessed and memorable time Lord, because of Your working in our hearts. Draw everything together and conclude things, we pray, Lord, and even if we forget many things, may Your abiding presence and the sense of Your speaking and working be with every one of us. Lord You know the days we are living in, and You know our need to hear what You are saying. Will You help us, Lord, to take in and not to misinterpret what You are saying to us? This we ask together in the name of our Lord Jesus, Amen.

The Climax of All History

As we come to the end, I have one last burden, which in one sense is certainly nothing profound and furthermore nothing new. However, I must say that I think I need to restate certain things and emphasize them in the light of the days in which we are living.

The most wonderful thing about the coming of the Lord Jesus is that it is the climax of all history. There is no way in which you and I can read the Word of God honestly and spiritualise away the coming of the Lord Jesus, as if it is some golden millennial age that is somehow going to descend upon this war-torn and weary unhappy world.

The Bible says quite clearly that in the same manner in which He went, He will return. Even a little child in the midst of that group of disciples who watched the Lord Jesus ascend into heaven and heard the words of the angels, "He shall come again in like manner," (Acts 1:11) would have understood that in the bodily way in which the Lord Jesus ascended into the glory, He would return to this earth. His feet would stand again upon the earth of this globe. His feet would stand upon the Mount of Olives in Jerusalem again. It is the climax of all history.

In His return all the glorious plans of God find their complete fulfilment. Indeed, I would go further and say that in my estimation, the atoning work of the Lord Jesus Christ is not really complete until He actually returns because it is then that we have our redemption bodies, and we shall be changed in the twinkling of an eye. In a flash we shall be changed, and we shall have bodies like His. In other words, the coming again of our Lord Jesus, the return of the Messiah, is the completion of the whole movement of God for salvation. Isn't that wonderful? It means that until He comes, there is something incomplete about you and me, and I can tell you right away what it is. It is that you and I have bodies that are decaying. We may have had spirits that have been justified and souls that are being won by His grace and by His working, but we still have bodies. There is going to come a day when they are going to be put away.

So complete, so full, so marvellous, so eternal is our salvation that it is not only a matter to do with spirit and to do with soul, it is a matter to do with our physical bodies. We are going to have a body like His. I can't wait for it. It excites me—the thought of going through walls and going up vertically and down and around, and all kinds of things like that. People get so excited about getting a man on the moon. What does it matter about getting a man on the moon or photographing the other side of Mars when we can have a body like His in another dimension of experience?

Now, the return of the Lord Jesus is the climax of all history. It is a very interesting fact, if I may just again underline it, that the Lord Jesus spoke more about His coming again than ever He did about His cross. Isn't that interesting? This does not devalue the work of the cross. Yet, if we are to look at the amount of material that He gave to us concerning His coming, it is far, far more than what He said about the cross. That is not to devalue the cross or the work of the cross, but what it means is this: until He returns, the work is incomplete! It is all part of a symphony and His coming again is the last movement of the symphony. It is the finale of the whole thing. Now surely that should lift up your heads and cause a little flash of some kind of ecstasy to go through your spirit. Even if there are persecutions, tribulations, distress, pressures, and I don't know what else that lies ahead, the very thought that we are so near to the completion of our salvation, to the coming of the kingdom of God, to a new heaven and a new earth wherein dwells righteousness ought, I say, to thrill us.

Matters of Certainty and Oneness

There are some things upon which we can be absolutely one about His coming. There is much controversy and much confusion and much difference of opinion concerning the coming again of our Lord Jesus. Yet upon certain matters we can be dogmatic and absolutely one. We can be unanimous. He is going to come back literally, and in the body in which He went, He will return with the marks in His hands and in His feet and in His side, glorified but there forever for every one of us to see. It is a glorious reminder of the cost of our salvation, and that so great love and mercy which has won every single one of us to Himself. That is the first thing.

The Final Vindication

The second thing is this: His coming again will be the final vindication that He is the Messiah, the Son of the living God. It will be the vindication of His person, the vindication of His work, and the vindication of His words. That, I think, is marvellous! Until then, people can argue, people can doubt, people can do what they want. However, when He comes, that will be the final vindication that God has given to us the Lord Jesus Christ, as the Saviour of the world, that there is salvation in none other name. For there was no other name given under heaven among men whereby men and women must be saved (Acts 4:12).

The Vindication of His Followers

Thirdly, it will be the vindication of all those who have followed Him. Oh, how often we have been tempted to compromise. How often we have been tempted to find an easier way. How often it would have been easier to tone down the proclamation of the truth, or to leave certain things out, or not to go the whole way with the Lord. But the coming again of the Lord Jesus will be the vindication of all those who have followed the Lamb whithersoever He has gone. For those who have paid the price, whatever the cost, to follow Him and to be uncompromising in every single aspect of their life, it will be their glorious vindication. Then, if we do cry, it will be tears of joy and tears of relief that God will have to wipe away from our faces. It will seem to us so stupid that we ever argued with God about the way that He led us, that we ever rebelled over the ways that He wanted us to go when He asked us to surrender something. We shall be so glad that the Spirit of God enabled us to let go of things, to do His will, to follow Him. We will not have a single regret.

Can you imagine seeing anyone there saying, "Oh, I do wish I had held on to that?" "I wish I had not really agreed to go that way with Him." Can you imagine it? We will not even talk about it! We shall just say, "Oh, the grace of God that got me in a corner! The grace of God that got me into a place where I had to surrender! The grace of God that followed me and almost pressurised me into going the whole way with Him. Oh, I am so thankful!" I think there will be many tears - many tears of relief, of joy at the very thought that God in His great love took us at our word and cornered us so that we had to go the whole way with Him.

It will be the vindication of all those who have followed Him. Think of all those who lost their lives. Think of brethren like Watchman Nee who spent over 20 years in prison. Oh, the vindication of these people in glory! Then their affliction will seem to have been, in the light of eternal weight of glory, just light affliction—transient and temporal—compared with the eternal and exceedingly great weight of glory which it has worked (II Corinthians 4:17). The vindication of all those who have followed Him.

The Vindication of the Word of God

Again, it will be the vindication of the Word of God. Oh, sometimes the Word of God seems so stupid. May I be forgiven, if it is misunderstood what I mean, but sometimes the Word of God seems so stupid, doesn't it? When we take Darwinian theory, it is so clever. It is so clever, seemingly so logical and look where it is leading the world! To abortion! There are more human beings that are beings destroyed in the United States than the third of the Jewish people who died in the Holocaust. Did you know that? Before Mr. Begin, may God bless him for it, abolished abortion in Israel, one million young Israeli lives had been exterminated— one-sixth of all our people who died in the Holocaust.

Oh, my dear friends, this Darwinian theory it seems so clever that we are just the evolution of matter. Somehow or other we have come up from some kind of primeval squelch or mulch or whatever else it was. They do not always say we are now descended from monkeys, but somehow or other we have come up from green slime and somehow we have moved upward and upward and upward and upward. If this present century is the result of moving upward and upward and upward, I think it would be good to move downward. With the millions and millions and millions and millions of people that have died at the hand of their fellow human beings in the most ghastly circumstances. Is this the upward process of evolution? It seems so clever doesn't it? Of course, the Nazis introduced abortion, they legalized abortion. Before very long they legalized euthanasia, mercy killing of the mentally ill, and of course, it led to genocide—the destruction of the Jewish people and, it is often forgotten, one and a half million gypsies. It would have led in the end to the destruction of the Slavic people.

Once you have agreed that man is nothing more than matter, he is not made in the image of God, he is not an individual in whom God has put something of eternity, you can destroy him and exterminate him. The coming again of the Lord Jesus will be the vindication of the Word of God that man *was* made in the image of God, that man *is* accountable and responsible to God, that *every* man must stand before God.

I use that as an illustration, yet there are many other things. The Word of God says many other things that at times run counter to modern philosophy and the attitudes of this world. At times, because of our education and our cultural background it is much easier to believe what happens to be the "in vogue" idea of today than the Word of God. But I will tell you this, the Word of God lives and abides forever. When these ideas have long since been discarded, God's Word is still the same, still as powerful, still as alive, still as creative as ever. Everything else passes away, but the Word of the Lord, that endures forever (1 Peter 1:24–25).

When the Lord Jesus returns, that Word of God will be vindicated before the nations of the world. Then the whole universe will know that the Word of God is truth and that it is eternal. Thank God for that! I have in my little life never seen a person whose life has been totally changed, turned inside out, renewed, and remade by a word of Shakespeare, or a word of Goethe, or a word of Confucius, or anybody else. They may have some marvellous things to say, and in fact at times it may be the insight of genius. However, I have never found a person born of God through a word of Shakespeare or joined into a union with the living God through some word of Goethe or Confucius. Yet, take this old book that people have despised, spoken against, contradicted, devalued and denigrated and what do you find, here in the 20th century? Some drug addict, into his heart comes a word from this Book and it saves the man and changes the man and remakes the man. Or an alcoholic that cannot be saved by anybody, into his heart by the Spirit of God comes this living and active Word of God, sharper than any two edged sword (Hebrews 4:12) and something happens in that life. Even if you and I have not got such dramatic experiences as being saved from alcoholism or drug addiction, have we not all known the Word of God coming alive and coming into our hearts? Sometimes this Book has so risen up that it almost hit me. Has it not done that to you, or am I alone in this kind of experience? When somehow something that you have known for years, suddenly, a phrase leaps out at you and catches you. You are never the same afterwards. Never again are you the same. Something has happened. It is the living and active Word of God, sharper than any two edged sword dividing between soul and spirit. This is the vindication of the Word of God.

The Universe in Harmony

There will also be the proof that only when God is King will the universe be in harmony. I cannot wait for that day when finally it is proved before the nations of the world that only when the Lord Jesus is King and Lord of all, when He is in the seat of government will this whole universe finally be harmonized. No more war. No more strife. No more corruption. No more decay. Absolute righteousness as the foundation of all government.

Oh, I cannot wait for the day when righteousness and truth are the basis of all government in this world instead of having to witness heads of state hugging and kissing killers, murderers, and assassins; giving them banquets and giving them fulsome and untrue tributes for the sake of coexistence. Oh, may that day come soon when we do not have to have coexistence with evil, when we do not have to sit down at a table and have a banquet with a man who has murdered hundreds of thousands of other human beings, when we do not have to have a president of the United States describing Mao as one of the greatest lights that ever shone in the East. Oh, may the day come when righteousness and truth and mercy and love are the foundation of government, when government is exercised on the basis of what is right and not what is politic or diplomatic.

Oh, that day is going to come when the King comes. He will be a King who will reign in righteousness. The sceptre of His throne is a sceptre of righteousness, not a kind of hard, heavy, dark thing that people associate with narrow-mindedness and bigotry, but something so broad, so loving, so universal, so magnificent in concept, but absolutely righteous and true. What a wonderful day we have to look forward to!

It is more than that. In that day when the Lord comes, the whole universe will suddenly flow in a harmony. The prophets can hardly contain themselves when they talk about this. They speak about a leopard and a kid feeding together and a lion eating straw like an ox. They speak about a little child playing with a cobra! Can you think of it? Putting its hand in the nest of vipers. Nothing in the whole of God's holy mountain will injure or harm, but the glory of the Lord will cover the earth as the waters cover the sea (Isaiah 11:6–9). Oh, what a marvellous day! What a marvellous day!

Of course, the apostle Paul speaks about it. He says, "The whole natural creation groans in the pain of childbirth, in travail, waiting for the manifestation of the glory of the children of God" (see Romans 8:22). Oh, how wonderful it will be when this old world, which even in its fallen and disharmonious state, "nature red in tooth and claw," as one hymn writer described it in a famous hymn—when this whole creation suddenly is released from its bondage to corruption and division and becomes what God intended it to be.

The prophets cannot contain themselves. They speak about fields and hills singing for joy. They speak about the trees of the woods and of the fields clapping their hands for joy when the Lord comes (Isaiah 55:12). You have never seen a tree clapping its hand have you? I don't think it means literally, but it means that this whole natural creation will burst out of its bondage. It is even now so beautiful in spite of its disharmony and its fall. Is it not so beautiful? What will it be when the King comes and the whole thing is released into what it was intended originally to be? Oh, how marvellous! The King!

The Coming Again of the Lord Jesus— Three Schools of Thought

There are many other things we could say that we are all absolutely one upon in this matter. But when we come to the actual coming again of the Lord Jesus, there are basically three different schools of thought. One is that the Lord Jesus will return, and it will be one movement. There will be no rapture, certainly no going before any tribulation. Everyone has to go through the tribulation according to this school of thought, of interpretation, and at the end the Lord will come. Now, this has an attractive simplicity about it. At a first reading it seems so very clear, so very logical, so very simple. We shall all go right through to the end. They say there are not two comings of the Lord, but only one. It also has the added advantage, if you like to call it an advantage, that the church fathers and the reformers all happened to believe this view of the coming again of the Lord Jesus.

There is a second view, which has now become a very widely held view amongst God's people. It began about two centuries ago, principally with the leaders of what have come to be known as the Christian Brethren, godly and remarkable men. That view is that if we look into the Word of God, we cannot accept that there is only one final movement because we are told on the one hand that He's going to come as a thief in a hidden way, in a stealthy way, in an unexpected way (1 Thessalonians 5:2), and on the other side we are told that he's going to come with blazing fire, trumpets blowing, the whole earth quaking, and that His sign will appear in the heavens. They say, "You see there seem to be two quite different sets of Scripture for His coming. How do you explain that?" They say that the Lord will come *for* His own and then He will come *with* His own.

Now I have to tell you, I think there are problems with both these views. If we take the first view we have very real problems. I cannot go into them because of time, and I do not wish to upset anybody who cherishes that first view because amongst us here there must be people who have come to their own satisfaction and peace of mind over one or the other of these views. I can only say this, for myself, if I want to be absolutely honest, I find real problems that cannot be explained away about that first school of interpretation. However, I have to tell you also that I have problems with the second school of interpretation as real as those of the first.

Oh, dear, now what do we do? About the same time as this second school of interpretation began to come into existence and began to gain acceptance, another view came, principally expounded by some quite remarkable men and teachers of the Word of God—D.M. Panton, G.H. Pember, G.H. Lang amongst them, T. Austin Sparks more latterly, and others who felt that both the former schools left much to be desired. They said that there will be two movements in the Lord's return. He will come *for* His own and He will come, in the end, *with* His own. They said, and this is the unique feature, only those who are ready will be taken. The rest will be left to go through the tribulation and will be purified in it. Now, some people say that this view creates more problems than it solves. However, I have to tell you that as far as I am concerned, I think it solves nearly all the problems. Having said that, I have to tell you that it is not problem-free. There are still some very real problems.

Now, I have always had a fear of what I call theories of adjustment, that is, you get a view and you bash the Scriptures into your view. You get a line and then you take the other things and somehow or other you push them and press them and finally you make them fall into line with whatever view you have adopted. May I say something that I hope will be of real help and not confusing? I suspect that if our Lord Jesus had really wanted us to have a cast-iron view of the details of His return, He would have given one short supplementary discourse in which He would have clearly stated exactly the sequence of the events, but He never did. Do you mean to tell me that He was not aware of some of the confusion that would result from what is said in the New Testament on this matter? Of course not. Therefore, I come to this conclusion that it is by design. It is by design. In other words, the Lord is more interested in His people walking by faith with Him with an ear open to the Spirit of God in the last days, than having a cast-iron system of what is called eschatology, that is, the events of the end.

Isn't it interesting that the Lord Jesus said, "Take heed, take heed, take heed, take heed, watch and pray, watch, be ready"? If you and I are really ready, does it matter? If we are ready and He only comes for those who are ready, we shall be taken. Thank God for that! If we are ready and He comes for all and takes all born again believers to be with Himself, thank God we are ready. We will not be ashamed. If we have to go through the distress and tribulation before His coming, at least to be ready will mean that we are prepared for whatever is coming. For me, I think the point of the matter is, be ready. I think it is a good thing to have honest convictions on this matter. I have my own convictions about the coming of the Lord. I personally believe the third view is the view that is the most Scriptural and, to me, the most obvious. But having said that, I will not divide from any brother or sister who feels differently to me on this matter of the coming of the Lord. I want to be open and loving and yet hold my convictions as you hold yours. What I want to see in you and what I want to find in myself is a readiness for His coming, not some dogmatic spirit on all the details of His coming in which we are factious and divisive, but a spirit of real love and openness and humility in which you and I can hold convictions concerning His return strongly, but not in a fierce spirit.

Take Heed/Be Ready

The one thing we can say is that He is coming. His coming is drawing nearer every day. People say, "Well, didn't the apostle Paul expect Him to come in his lifetime?" Yes. Well then, it must be much nearer than it was then, that is all I can say. People seem to think because the apostle Paul thought He was coming back in his lifetime, we should discard the whole idea. What nonsense! Does anyone come nearer to the Lord Jesus and who is not quickened by the thought of His coming? Once you come near to the eternal, it is as if His coming is right on the brink because you have left time for the dimension of eternity. I can quite understand how in different ages people have thought the that Lord is coming. The only thing I have to say is that today we not only have the fulfilment of certain signs, but we have that one unique sign concerning the Jewish people, which is the confirmation of all the others.

So now let me sum up further. What is the vital need for us all? What does it mean to be ready? Because it is this readiness which is the priority; all else is secondary. How we see the coming of the Lord and the details of it, in actual fact is secondary to the question of being ready. Our Lord could have solved this whole matter as I have said, by a few well-chosen words, but instead He used His breath to say: Take heed, take heed, take heed. Be on your guard, be alert, be alive, be watchful, be awake, be ready.

Settle the Issues in Your Life

There are three things, spiritually at least, which I believe we need to take heed to and give attention to if we are going to be ready. The first is the Holy Spirit must be allowed to settle the many issues in our lives whatever the cost. Oh, let me again emphasise this. I said something about it before, but let me say it again. You will never regret allowing the Holy Spirit to settle the issues in your lives, today. I have never met a person who has come to me and said, "I am so sorry that I settled that issue with God." I have found many people who have come to me and said, "I have wasted ten years of my life because I never settled that issue that God was speaking to me about."

Now the issues may be all kinds of things. It may be something in your life God is telling you to give up. It may be so small. You know, it can be such a small thing as handball, or basketball, or even swimming. Now do not get me wrong. It is not as if God is saying, "Swimming is wrong." That would be nonsense. But sometimes because God is disciplining you, He says, "You know this thing that means so much to you? I want you to give it to Me." Then we start to argue, "Don't be silly, don't be silly. There is nothing wrong in that. Chewing candy, what is wrong in that?" But it is not chewing candy or swimming or whatever else, it is your *obedience*. A straw tells which way the wind is blowing. That is why sometimes enormous spiritual experience, life-changing in its influence and power, hinges on a small issue in your life that seems to be totally insignificant.

Sometimes the issues may be other things. Maybe God is calling you into service somewhere in some difficult part of the earth and you are at present not very willing. Or maybe it is that the Lord wants you to commit yourself to those brothers and sisters in real fellowship and you are on the periphery of it all the time. You can see all the faults and failings of those brothers and sisters, and you say, "Oh, if they were only better. If they were only larger, or they were more spiritual, or something else and God is saying deep down in your heart, "Commit yourself, commit yourself, commit yourself," but you say, "How can I commit myself? They are such a grotty lot. I mean they are so poor, they are so insignificant, they are so little. Why should *I* commit myself to them?" However, on the issue of your committal to the Lord Jesus in your poor brothers and sisters, a lot depends.

Do you know that is the principle of Bethlehem? Our Lord Jesus faced just that issue. When somewhere in eternity the Father said, "Who will go for Me? And whom shall I send?" It could have been the Lord Jesus said, "What? Born in those circumstances? To that lot? They do not care. They do not want Me. They are not very spiritual. You mean that I have got to be born of a human being into that kind of circumstance? The Lord may be calling on you to go into such circumstances—circumstances of limitation, circumstances that apparently are full of insignificance, committing yourself to little people, with petty problems and very little horizon. Yet, God in your heart is saying, "You will come out of it, if You follow Me, with a wider horizon and a greater character."

You see dear brothers and sisters, the one thing that matters with God is not knowledge, but character. Character is all-important as far as God is concerned. He does not want the Kingdom of God to be peopled with countless multitudes of characterless babes. They have no character. Nothing has ever been developed in them. He wants people likened to His Son with characters that have been developed and expanded and somehow matured by the things which they suffered. Issues that God speaks to you about, only you can face and say, "Yes," to Him. Sometimes, if I may so say from my own experience, if you cannot be honest and cannot say,

"I will," why not ask Him to make you willing to be willing? That might be the first step in a direction in your life that will end in unimaginable blessing.

So, if you are going to be ready, you and I have got to settle issues. Sometimes the issues are in our own heart. Sometimes it is to do with service. Sometimes it is to do with the fellowship of God's people. Sometimes it is that God is calling you to do a humble bit of work in your assembly, in the assembly of God's people, and you would prefer a platform ministry. Or perhaps you feel you are qualified for a platform ministry and yet in your heart, God is asking you to do such a mundane little job, that you know very well nobody will ever take notice of. As another has said before, it is all like the hidden part of an iceberg, only God sees. But you know when the Lord comes, there will not be a single cup of water that has been given in His name that will go unrewarded. There is not a single bit of service unseen, overlooked, hidden, that has not been noted by our Lord. It is precisely such service that brings us to the throne. Issues.

Sometimes, we may have collisions. I would like to know if there is anybody reading this who has not had a collision with another human being. If so, I would love to meet you. Indeed, the more will you have got, the more personality you have got, and the more strength of character you have got, probably the more collisions you have had. Some of the issues are just to humble ourselves before one another.

You know, the Lord spoke about washing the saints' feet. Do you know whose job it was to wash the saints' feet? It was the most menial of slaves in the household. It was their job to be at the entrance of the courtyard of the house and as soon as anybody came in from the dusty highways or paths, to wash their feet in cool water. Sometimes the water had rose petals in it because feet, as you probably all know, are somewhat smelly. Wouldn't it have been nicer if the Lord had said, "Shake the hands of your brother and sister," or "put your hand on their shoulder and say, 'Praise the Lord,'"? I know many people who put their hands on the shoulders of brothers and sisters and say, "Praise the Lord," and it doesn't mean a thing. To wash someone's smelly feet means you have to stoop. You cannot get somebody to stand up here so that you can remain standing and erect whilst you wash their feet. To wash another brother's or sister's feet means you have to stoop before them. It is as simple as that.

You know it is strange how we find a rigidity in us when it comes to washing one another's feet. It is not so easy to humble ourselves before one another, not so easy to put something right, not so easy to ask for forgiveness. Of course, sometimes we can do it in a very, very spiritual way. You know we go to someone and we say, "I wish to ask your forgiveness, but you were so awful, and you are so difficult that you have got me down. But the Lord has spoken to me and I am coming now to ask your forgiveness, even though I know you are the same."

I have seen many such so-called reconciliations where people put the knife in in a very spiritual way and go to someone else to get some irritation off their chest. It would be much better to have it out with someone and say, "You know I find you extremely irritating. I wonder whether you and I could get on our knees together?" That would at least be honest, but I don't even know whether that is what the Lord wants. It's not washing the saints' feet, is it? That I think is throwing a bowl of cold water in their face. However, if God could only deal with you so that you are humble, and you are broken, maybe you would forget the other person with all their awkwardness and difficulty and for the first time you could see them as a means of glory and grace. Issues.

Take Up Your Cross

If we're going to be ready, we not only need to allow the Holy Spirit to settle these issues in our hearts, but we must take up our cross. To be ready, you must take up your cross. What does it mean when the Lord Jesus said, "If any man would come after me, let him deny himself, take up his cross and follow me"? (Matthew 16:24). It would be so much easier if he had said, "If any man would follow me let him deny himself, take up *the* cross and follow me." Some people think that a migraine headache is their cross. Or a painful hip is their cross. Or some awkward wife is their cross. Or some grumpy husband is their cross. Or difficult children are their cross. Or some very demanding boss is their cross. This is to devalue the work of the cross altogether.

What did the Lord Jesus mean when He said, "If any man would follow Me, let him deny himself, take up his cross and follow Me."? You know, they never did take up a whole cross. In the old days, the stake was left in the ground. They took the crossbeam. Whenever you saw a man going through the streets of Jerusalem, hauling on his back that crossbeam, it meant he was as good as dead. His opinions did not matter anymore. His circumstances did not matter anymore. The difficulties he had with relationships did not matter anymore. He was a dead man.

It was Tozer who said, "When a man is crucified, he cannot walk backwards. For the first time, he can only look in one direction."

"If any man would follow Me, let him deny himself and take up his sentence of death and come after Me." God has sentenced you to death, so why do you fight for your rights? One of the new versions puts it very simply, very directly. It puts it like this: "If any man would follow Me, let him give up all right to himself, take up his cross, and come after Me."

The matter of rights is the big thing today—rights, rights, rights—women's rights, men's rights, the rights of this colour, the rights of that colour, the rights of this nationality, the rights of that nationality, of this race, of that race—rights, rights, rights, rights. This whole thing has got right into the church because it awakens something in us that is already very powerful: I. "I have rights! I am not going to be bossed around, I am not going to be directed, I am not going to be trampled on, I am not going to be used as a doormat. If anyone thinks they can push me around or push me in a corner, they have another think coming! I have rights!"

The heart of the gospel is this: If any man follow Me, let him give up all right to himself, take up his cross, and come after Me. If you once saw that God has sentenced your old man or woman to death, then I think you will suddenly realise, what do opinions really matter? Does it matter if someone has got the wrong idea of your reputation, that someone besmirches you anymore? You are a dead person.

You and I can never be ready for the coming of the Lord or for what is coming on the face of the earth, unless you and I lay down our lives. Otherwise our treasures will be in ourselves, in our circumstances, in our possessions, and not in the Lord. We are so wedded to these things that it is only when we give up all right to ourself that we can be severed from them. It does not mean that you should not have possessions, but it does mean you should not grasp hold of them.

Can you imagine what lies ahead of us in the days of the future, if you and I are still self-centred, selfish, self-seeking, and self-interested? Can you imagine? We are not safe people! The enemy has only to play upon our fear and when it comes to a question of death or compromise, we will compromise to save our skins. If it comes to a question of a choice between an easier way and a harder way, we will choose the easier way because we have not given up all right to ourselves and taken up our cross and followed Him.

There is no way for character to be developed in the believer except through the work of the cross. No child of God has gone very far until he finds in his way stark, bloody, and inescapable, the cross of the Lord Jesus. When that time comes, you either go through with Him into a new dimension of Christian living and life and power, or you go out of the way into a side path where you will remain for forty years in the wilderness, going round and round—singing the same hymns, saying the same prayers, having the same problems, and really getting nowhere. Oh, you will have manna, six days out of seven, and water out of the rock, and a pillar of cloud and fire to guide you, but you will never come into the promised land. God does not forsake you. But you chose it, not He.

"If any man follow me, let him give up all right to himself, take up his cross and follow Me." We are not safe for these days that lie ahead, unless we know something of the cross in our lives. How can we begin to explore and experience the fathomless and unsearchable riches of the Lord Jesus unless first we have been divorced from our own self-confidence, our own energies, and our own talents? There is no other way.

The Anointing of the Holy Spirit and His Fullness

Let me say something else, if you and I are going to be ready for the coming of the Lord, we need to have an experience of the anointing of the Holy Spirit and His fullness. There is no other way. Many years ago, when we were talking about the end, I asked Mr. Sparks: "What do you think will characterise the very last days for the people of God?" He said, "Well, funnily enough, many, many years ago, when I was young, I asked A.B. Simpson the same question. He said, 'The one thing that will characterise the last part of the age will be a rediscovery of the person and work of the Holy Spirit.'"

I have no doubt about that. Nothing else will carry God's people through the last phase and enable them to overcome than a dynamic experience of the anointing and power of the Holy Spirit. When people tell me they are afraid of too dramatic an experience, I do not know what is wrong with them. We need supernatural power and grace for supernatural conditions. The Bible says that in the last days, demons will flood the whole earth. The darkness will cover it. That many other workings of Satan using miracles and signs and great dramatic displays of power will deceive even the elect if it be possible. We need the anointing and fullness of the Holy Spirit.

My brothers and sisters, do not be afraid of any experience of the Holy Spirit. Seek God that He may immerse you in the Holy Spirit. There is nothing more wonderful than to be lost in the person of the Holy Spirit much more than for the Holy Spirit to be trapped in you. The way some people speak it seems like they have the Holy Spirit, but I think it would be much more wonderful if the Holy Spirit got you.

People say, "Well, just wait. I don't want to get unbalanced. I don't want to become extreme. I don't want to become wild." Are you telling me that God the Holy Spirit will make you unbalanced, extreme, and wild? Just because some people behave in a very unfortunate manner and call it the work of the Holy Spirit does not mean that the Holy Spirit will make you wild, and extreme, and unbalanced, and offensive! When the Holy Spirit gets hold of a human being, He beautifies them. He takes their education in hand and starts to break them. When the Holy Spirit gets hold of somebody, he starts to put His finger on all kinds of things in their lives. He starts to cause light to shine in dark places. There is nothing to fear with the Holy Spirit. He is like a dove - so gentle, so sensitive, and at the same time He is fire. He will burn up all the chaff and all the dross. Do not be afraid of the Holy Spirit.

Let me tell you this, if you and I have no experience of the Holy Spirit, we are going to have a very hard time in the days that lie ahead, believe you me. When we do not have our own experience of the Holy Spirit we have to depend on leaders. We have to get our direction from other saints. We are all the time saying, "I don't know the will of God. Would you please tell me how should I do this. Should I go this way? Should I go that way? Please explain it to me."

People phone a thousand miles and say to a brother, "Brother, would you tell me, shall I take this job or shall I not?" Isn't that a lot of nonsense, when in the Word of God it says about the sign of the new covenant that every one of them shall know the Lord from the least to the greatest? Of course, you should have fellowship, but only when you think you know what the Lord wants for you. Then, when you have got something clear, you go to your brethren and say, "Now, tell me do you think I'm right in doing this? This is what I think the Lord wants for me." We need the Holy Spirit. May God help us in this matter.

The Duties of a Watchman

Well now dear friends, I think our time is gone, but let me finish with these words about watchmen. The Lord Jesus ended these words of this major discourse on His coming again with the words, "And what I say to you I say to all, watch." Are we only to watch for our own lives? I do not think so. What are the duties of a watchman? The duties of a watchman are to guard the interests of the king and of the city. He must remain awake whilst others sleep. He has to spot from afar any movements that could injure the interests of the king and the city. Therefore, the one great requirement in a watchman is the ability to stay awake. What good is a watchman if he is always falling asleep?

The second thing about a watchman is that he must have one hundred percent vision. You do not have blind watchmen.

He must be able to spot with his eyes a single movement that might be the beginning of an assault upon the city.

Brothers and sisters, you and I are watchmen. Does it not say in Isaiah 62:6–7, "I have set watchmen upon your walls, O Jerusalem; they shall never hold their peace day nor night: ye that love the Lord's remembrancers, take no rest and give him no rest, till he establish and till He make Jerusalem a praise in the whole earth"?

It was to Ezekiel that God said: Son of Man, I have made you watchman over this nation, to the whole house of Israel. If when I say judgment is coming and you sound the alarm and blow the trumpet, and that man does not take heed of you and dies, he died in his sin. You have saved yourself. But, if you do not blow the trumpet or sound the alarm, and judgment comes and takes that man away, his blood will I require at your hand (see Ezekiel 33:7–8).

Dear people of God, we have a solemn God-given responsibility for the world in which we are found. We, that is the church of the Lord Jesus Christ, wherever she may be found, all over this earth, we are the only community in the Earth who has a knowledge of what is going to happen. We are the only community in the whole world that can blow a trumpet and sound the alarm. Unfortunately, because we are also frightened of the word of prophecy, it has become the realm of the lunatic fringe, and the domain of eccentrics and of cults. The result is they have moved anywhere that the church of God should have been entrenched, and they are the ones who are all the time talking about this or that or the other. Shame upon us when the Mormons are prepared for three years of siege, every single Mormon family, and yet real believers seem to think they don't have to do a single thing about anything! When Russellites, Jehovah's witnesses, so-called, are more aware that we are in the last days than are the people of God themselves. It is because we have become so afraid of the extremists and the eccentrics, we have withdrawn from the whole subject of prophecy, and we have left it to the realm of cults and eccentrics.

This does not mean that God will not require the blood of the nation at the hands of the Church, if they have not warned people, not just by word of mouth but by their very conduct, by their behaviour, by their mode of living. By something within them that God has done, they become a prophetic community, a prophetic witness to the world. There is a little phrase in a prophecy in Isaiah, which I am not sure is often rightly applied, but it is in Isaiah 21:11–12: "One calleth unto me out of Seir. 'Watchmen, what of the night? Watchmen, what of the night?' The watchmen said, 'The morning cometh and also the night.'"

Thank God, a morning is coming. That dawn of God's day is that upon which the whole Word of God focuses. When it tells us about the night coming and the things of the night—of darkness, of dragons and serpents and beasts and false prophets, and harlot churches and Babylon with all its splendour and glory, it does not bring all this before our gaze to make us fearful. It does not in fact focus attention on those things of the night. Those things of the night are passing. They are temporal. The word of prophecy focuses all our attention upon the coming of the day of God. That day of glory, that day of power, that day of vindication, that day of joy, that day when the redeemed will return to Zion with laughter in their mouths. That is the day upon which the whole Word of God focuses attention.

Be Ready

Brothers and sisters, we have a night before us. We do not know how much of the night we must pass through. Certainly, in my estimation, we have to pass through a little of it. For if I understand the words of the apostle Paul in his second letter to the Thessalonians, we have to see at least the beginning of the appearance of the man of sin before the Lord takes us. If that is so, we have some of the night to endure. Are we ready? Are we prepared? Are we alive? Are we awake? The night will pass, but the day of the Lord is forever. That is the issue. Are you and I living in the light of that day, as if it might come tomorrow? Ready for His coming, ready for His use, ready to be witnesses, whether in life or in death? God is calling us. We do not know how much time we have.

People come to me and say that I have said we have twenty years. Some come to me and say I have said we have four years. Others come to me and tell me that I said we have seven years. I do not recall ever saying we have four years, seven years, or twenty years. I may have said I thought there would be a world war within a certain period of time. I don't know when the Lord is going to come. I know He is coming. I don't know when He is coming, but I do know this: it could be tonight. I personally think we have a little more to go through, but it could be tonight because I could be wrong. It could be tonight, so there is only one thing to do: get ready.

Do not allow that strange spirit that is in all human beings to take you over: "Well, I think I'll do something about this next week. Tomorrow. Mañana." Tomorrow, tomorrow, tomorrow,

tomorrow. Tomorrow never comes. You will suddenly find that a week becomes a month, a month becomes a year, a year becomes five years, and five years becomes ten years, and still you are in the same condition you are in today. The Lord will have come before you will be ready. So let us get right and be ready, and more than ready. Let us be those that are watchmen God can use to awaken others, and to help others, and to bring others to Himself. May God help us to be ready, personally, to be part of the fellowship of God's people, in which we are getting ready together, and in a world in which we are holding forth the word of life, to multitudes around us who do not know where they are going or what is happening.

Other books by Lance Lambert can be found on lancelambert.org

"If Any Man Would Follow Me ..."

Battle for Israel

Be Ye Ready: Imperatives for Being Ready for Christ

Called Unto His Eternal Glory

Evangelism

Ezra - Nehemiah - Esther

Fellowship

Gathering Together Volume 1: Christian Fellowship

Gathering Together Volume 2: Christian Testimony

God Wants a House

How the Bible Came to Be: Part 1

How the Bible Came to Be: Part 2

In the Day of Thy Power

Jacob I Have Loved

Lessons from the Life of Moses

Let the House of God Be Built: The Story and Testimony of Halford House

Living Faith

Love Divine

My House Shall Be a House of Prayer

Preparation for the Coming of the Lord

Qualities of God's Servants

Reigning with Christ

Spiritual Character

Talks with Leaders

The Battle of the Ages

The Eternal Purpose of God

The Glory of Thy People Israel

The Gospel of the Kingdom

The Importance of Covering

The Last Days and God's Priorities

The Prize

The Relevance of Biblical Prophecy

The Silent Years

The Supremacy of Jesus

The Uniqueness of Israel

The Way to the Eternal Purpose of God

They Shall Mount up with Wings

Thine Is the Power

Thou Art Mine

Through the Bible with Lance Lambert: Genesis - Deuteronomy

Till the Day Dawns

*Unity : Behold How Good and How Pleasant
- Ministries from Psalm 133*

Warring the Good Warfare

What Is God Doing?: Lessons from Church History

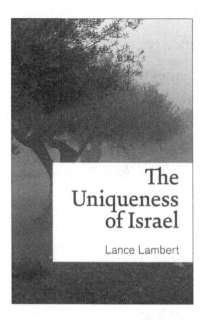

The Uniqueness of Israel

Woven into the fabric of Jewish existence there is an undeniable uniqueness. There is bitter controversy over the subject of Israel, but time itself will establish the truth about this nation's place in God's plan. For Lance Lambert, the Lord Jesus is the key that unlocks Jewish history He is the key not only to their fall, but also to their restoration. For in spite of the fact that they rejected Him, He has not rejected them.

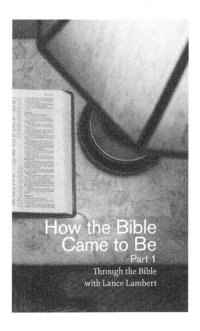

How the Bible Came to Be: Part 1

How is the Bible still as applicable in the 21st century as it was when it was first penned? How did so many authors, with different backgrounds and over thousands of years, write something so perfectly fitting with one another?

Lance Lambert breaks down these, and many other questions in this first volume of his series teaching through the Bible. He lays a firm foundation for going on to study the Word of the living God.

And ye shall seek me, and find me, when ye shall search for me
with all your heart.
Jeremiah 29:13

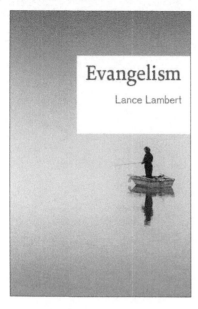

Evangelism
Lance Lambert

Evangelism

What is God's purpose in evangelism?

It is clear that the Word of God commands us to preach the gospel to every creature, to go into the whole world and make disciples of all nations baptising them in the name of the Father, the Son and the Holy Spirit.

So how do we do it?

In "Evangelism" Lance opens the scriptures to reveal how the church can practically and effectively preach the gospel to the unsaved world, by revealing to them in scripture their need for a Saviour, the work of the Saviour, and how to receive the Saviour. He explains practical means of winning souls and how to follow-up with the newly saved to make disciples of the Lord Jesus. Evangelism is the way by which we gather the materials for the house of God.

So faith comes by hearing, and hearing through the word of Christ.

Ezra-Nehemiah-Esther

"The Bible is not a history book. History is only found in the Scripture when it has something to teach us." (page 62)

Recovery. This key theme throughout the entire timeline of Ezra to Esther gives us a clear vision of the Lord's goal with His people. From the building of Jerusalem and its surrounding walls in Ezra and Nehemiah to the fixing of the irreversible decree of the annihilation of Jews in Esther, the Lord is contsantly using His people for recovery. In this book of the series, "Through the Bible with Lance Lambert," we find an indepth analysis of Ezra, Nehemiah, and Esther, tracing the workings of the Lord througout history.

Made in the USA
Middletown, DE
26 May 2022

66241299R00096